Whistle

Also by C. Fred Alford

Think No Evil: Korean Values in the Age of Globalization, 1999

What Evil Means to Us, 1997

The Man Who Couldn't Lie: Essays and Stories about an Ancient Quarrel between Philosophy and Poetry, 1995

Group Psychology and Political Theory, 1994

The Psychoanalytic Theory of Greek Tragedy, 1992

The Self in Social Theory: A Psychoanalytic Account of Its Construction in Plato, Hobbes, Locke, Rousseau, and Rawls, 1991

Melanie Klein and Critical Social Theory: An Account of Politics, Art, and Reason Based on Her Psychoanalytic Theory, 1989

Narcissism: Socrates, the Frankfurt School, and Psychoanalytic Theory, 1988

Science and the Revenge of Nature: Marcuse and Habermas, 1985

Ashes of the Moon: Environment and Evil in the Amazon, 2000 (a novel)

blowers

Broken Lives and Organizational Power

C. Fred Alford

Cornell University Press : Ithaca and London

First published 2001 by Cornell University Press
First printing, Cornell Paperbacks, 2002

Printed in the United States of America

Library of Congress Cataloging-in-Publication Data

Alford, C. Fred.
    Whistleblowers : broken lives and organizational power/C. Fred Alford.
        p.   cm.
    Includes bibliographical references and index.
    ISBN-13: 978-0-8014-8780-4 (pbk.: alk. paper)
    1. Whistle blowing. 2. Business ethics. 3. Administrative agencies—Corrupt practices.
4. Whistle bowing—Case studies. 5. Employees—Dismissal of—case studies. I. Title
    HD60 .A394 2001
    331.2—dc21

                                        00-011829

Cornell University Press strives to use environmentally responsible suppliers and materials to the
fullest extent possible in the publishing of its books. Such materials include vegetable-based,
low-VOC inks, and acid-free papers that are recycled, totally chlorine-free, or partly composed of
nonwood fibers. For further information, visit our website at www.cornellpress.cornell.edu.

Paperback printing   10 9 8 7 6 5 4 3

To the Whistleblowers

Contents

Preface

O N E of the first things I ever heard a whistleblower say was, "I've learned two things from being what you might call a professional whistleblower. When you go out in public, don't cry, and don't talk like your hair is on fire. If you do, no one will listen. It makes them uncomfortable."

The whistleblower who said this was at a conference on the future of whistleblowing. Not a single panel had a current whistleblower on it, though at least a dozen whistleblowers were in the audience. Several asked why there were no whistleblowers on the panels.

The answer, I believe, is that even the supporters of whistleblowers are afraid of the tears, the screams, the pain, and the horror; this fear teaches the whistleblower to subvert these experiences in the name of effective lobbying. There is a time and a place for that, of course, but I think we will not understand what is happening in our society until we listen to the tears, the screams, the pain, and the horror of those who have crossed a boundary they did not even know exists.

I began my research thinking I wanted to know why whistleblowers did it. I still do, and chapters 4 and 5, on whistleblower ethics, explore the issue. Why whistleblowers do it is not, however, the most important question. It may be a diversion if it keeps us from learning about the world from the whistleblower, as though interrogation were a substitute for listening. The most important question is what whistleblowers have learned about the world from their experience. "What kind of world do you inhabit so that this is who you became through your actions?" would be the ideal question, if anyone could answer it.

Since so much of this book is organized around my reactions to whistleblowers' accounts of their experiences, I should tell you how I came to know them. My first step was to attend a support group for whistleblowers. There I spent almost one hundred hours with a group of about a dozen whistleblowers. Most of the time I listened to whistleblowers talk among themselves. In addition, I attended a country retreat for stressed-out whistleblowers. Once again, most of the time was spent listening to whistleblowers talk with each other. I was not a participant observer, just an observer, even if some whistleblowers thought I knew more or could do more than I knew or could. I have also interviewed about two dozen whistleblowers, several of them for hours on different occasions.

In addition, many whistleblowers have their own web sites. I have visited dozens of sites, corresponded by e-mail with many of the whistleblowers who created these sites, talked with others on the telephone, and met several. A couple of web sites are devoted to whistleblowing in general. I advertised my interest in whistleblowers on an especially popular one (as measured by its "hits") and have been called or e-mailed by fourteen whistleblowers. Most whistleblowers love to tell their tales.

I have also been interviewed by several reporters, to whom I gladly give quotable quotes, primarily because these generate more mail from whistleblowers. Whistleblowers are dying to be listened to. In the Appendix, I discuss some of the problems raised by this fact, especially the problem of confidentiality.

In addition, thousands of whistleblower/whistleblowing entries are on the web, and many are fascinating. One web site holds the advisory decisions of the National Society of Professional Engineers' Board of Ethical Review, a marvelous resource.

I have attended a conference concerned with whistleblowing.

I am fortunate to have as a neighbor a psychologist whose practice is confined to whistleblowers. We have talked at length, and he has put me in touch with several of his clients by giving my name to them. I have a similar relationship with an attorney in Washington, D.C., whose practice consists largely of whistleblowers.

All unattributed quotations are from my research with whistleblowers.

I do not use a tape recorder, a practice I have adhered to through four books. Subjects never get used to the recorder; it always structures the conversation. Many whistleblowers would not have spoken to the tape recorder (especially at group meetings, where it would not have been allowed), though one whistleblower recorded our conversation for his own purposes. Still, I do not want to turn my rejection of the tape recorder into an unalloyed virtue. Because I rely on contemporaneous notes, I can capture only short quotations verbatim.

I regret that a couple of whistleblowers with whom I shared this manuscript were insulted, or at least put off, by my explanation of their whistleblowing as "narcissism moralized." As far as I can tell, narcissism moralized is the leading motive of Socrates, Saint Augustine, and Gandhi, among others. In my book, that's good company to be in.

I would like to thank the Government Accountability Project (GAP), which does more for whistleblowers than just about any other group. GAP understands that whistleblowing is a political act. Thomas Devine is the legal director of GAP, and Rod Frey organized the whistleblower support group I attended.

Should any reader of this book be looking for more practical advice, I recommend *The Whistleblower's Survival Guide: Courage without Martyrdom*, by Thomas Devine (1997).

Donald Soeken helped me better understand the experience of whistleblowing. To many whistleblowers he is a rock. Soeken would not agree with all of my conclusions.

My promise of confidentiality prevents me from thanking by name those who helped me most, the whistleblowers who shared their experiences with me. This book is dedicated to them.

My brother-in-law Ira Wolfson first directed me to the literature on rescuers, giving me a copy of *Conscience and Courage*, by Eva Fogelman.

My wife, Elly, attended the whistleblowers retreat with me and helped me understand their pain.

The Committee for Politics, Philosophy, and Public Policy at the University of Maryland, College Park, allowed me to present my thoughts on whistleblowers' ethics to them.

Guy Adams invited me to present some of my work on whistleblowers to the Association for Practical and Professional Ethics, and together with Michael Diamond invited me to publish an article on whistleblowing in a special edition of *American Behavioral Science*, which they edited.

Elizabeth Kiss, director of the Kenan Ethics Program at Duke University, invited me to speak about whistleblowers at a conference sponsored by the Kenan Program.

James Phelan, editor of *Narrative*, worked diligently with me on a piece I submitted to the journal, teaching me much about the study of narrative.

Each of these opportunities helped me refine my argument.

Among the whistleblowers I shared this manuscript with was Daniel Ellsberg, probably the most well-known whistleblower of them all, the one who released the Pentagon Papers. He worries that my emphasis on the trials and tribulations of whistleblowers might discourage future whistleblowers. I hope not. The world needs more, not fewer, whistleblowers. Though I tell a dark story about the costs of whistleblowing, the harsh reality is in some ways less terrifying than the inchoate dread of what might happen were one to step over some invisible line that defines belonging to the organization. Many whistleblowers would not do it again, but some would. This includes Ellsberg. The readiness to tell the truth at whatever cost to oneself may be a source of tremendous power for change. Not always, perhaps not often, but sometimes. For some that's enough.

C. FRED ALFORD

College Park, Maryland

CHAPTER 1

Introduction

Be loyal to the story. – Isak Dinesen

ALMOST twenty books on whistleblowing are available through Amazon.com, and more than a hundred articles have been published on the topic. Many of these include case studies. They tell an inspiring story of noble people with strong morals who stand up for what is true and just. They suffer substantial retaliation, and while most are vindicated, a few are not. But even those who are not triumphant in the end know they did the right thing. They are richer and better for the experience, even if it will always pain them. Almost all would do it again.

This has not been my experience as I have listened to whistleblowers tell their tales. Most are in some way broken, unable to assimilate the experience, unable, that is, to come to terms with what they have learned about the world. Almost all say they wouldn't do it again – if they had a choice, that is. John Brown put it this way:

> If I had to do it over again, I wouldn't blow the whistle for a million dollars. It ruined my life. My neighbor kept talking about all these stories he'd read about "the little man who stood up against the big corporation and won." Well, I stood up against the big corporation and I lost. I didn't just lose my job. I lost my house, and then I lost my family. I don't even see my kids anymore. My ex-father-in-law said if I'd been a real whistleblower I'd have been on 60 *Minutes*.
>
> I spent $50,000 to have my day in court, only it was more like my minute in court. After five years of waiting to get to court, the judge said I didn't have standing to sue. I was out on the street an hour after I walked in the door. I still owe my lawyer.

I

My boss, the one who told me to lie to the FBI. He got a promotion. You know what I do now? I deliver pizza. Me, a licensed professional engineer. The Engineers Association, they just wished me luck, said they admired someone who stood up for his beliefs. Take that to the bank. They wouldn't even help me find a new job. Nobody understands. Lots of people say they admire my spunk, but nobody has any idea of the consequences. No one wants to know.

So, I think I was crazy to blow the whistle. Only I don't think I ever had a choice. It was speak up or stroke out. So all I can really say is that I wouldn't do it again if I didn't have to. But maybe I'd have to. I don't know.

Most whistleblowers sound more like John Brown than the mythical whistleblowers of the case studies. It is interesting to ask why. Those who write these case studies do not intend to mislead. They have, I believe, listened too much to the content, not enough to the narrative form. It is in the interpenetration of content and form (form as content, content as form) that one comes closest to grasping the affliction of the whistleblower. Most often this affliction is expressed as an odd disconnection between the narrator and his or her story. John Brown is unusual in this regard, more connected than most to his travail. In an attempt to think more systematically about the relationship between form and content in whistleblowers' stories, I have from time to time turned to the study of narrative.

Though I've interviewed whistleblowers at length, most of my time has been spent listening to whistleblowers tell their stories to each other, which is why this is an account of their narratives. The whistleblower support group I attended for almost a year was run a little bit like Alcoholics Anonymous, in which the price of admission was one's story.

The whistleblower retreat that I attended at the farm of a former whistleblower had the quality of an encounter group. The price of admission was still one's story, but the stories of many whistleblowers sounded a little different way out in the country late at night, though perhaps I had changed after several days and nights listening to their stories.

If the price of admission to the whistleblower support group was one's story, then should I tell you my story to entice you to read my book? All I can tell you is that I have never been a whistleblower, and yet I've felt like one all my life. In my family no one ever spoke the truth, so I thought I must. Of course, it wasn't the truth, just my truth, but that counts for something. In my profession, people tell lots of tiny truths, and so it has seemed important to me to try to tell big ones, even if that makes it harder to get it right. The big difference between my situation and that of the whistleblower is that I work in a remarkably tolerant profession, practicing it in a remarkably accommodating academic department. I can say almost anything and be ignored. Perhaps this is why I became so interested in what whistleblowers learned when their truths were taken so seriously, when, in other words, their truths were experienced as a threat to power.

WHAT THE SCAPEGOAT KNOWS

Let us call this whistleblower I am talking about the last man. Not Nietzsche's last man, who wants nothing more than a comfortable existence, but George Orwell's (1949, 222) last man in *Nineteen Eighty-Four*, Winston Smith, who sacrifices everything for a little piece of "ownlife." Exposed and tortured by O'Brien, Winston Smith is finally placed before a three-paneled mirror, the kind one finds in clothing stores so one can see if the suit fits. Pale, naked, looking like a skeleton, missing some teeth, Smith doesn't recognize himself for a moment. Says O'Brien, "If you are a man, Winston, you are the last man. Your kind is extinct." The whistleblower is the last man, not just tortured but exposed and sacrificed so that others might see what it costs to be an individual in this benighted world.

Contemporary social theory takes one of two forms. Either it posits the autonomous individual, leading to all the objections of Michel Foucault and others that such an individual is a fiction. Or the theory assumes that the autonomous individual does not exist, which is Foucault's position, even as he finds sources of resistance in the body, the same place Winston Smith found his.

What if the autonomous individual exists, but the organization cannot stand it, mobilizing vast resources in the service of the individual's destruction? (Society may not be able to stand it either, but it is not so organized and vindictive.) If this were so, then neither liberal social theory nor Foucault could see it. One would find something that barely exists; the other would be unable to discover the traces of what has been destroyed. Rather than assume that the individual exists, or does not, it may be more fruitful to focus on the ceremonies of his destruction. Consider the possibility that the individual destroyed is still an individual. Indeed, the individual destroyed is the best archaeological evidence of individuality's clandestine presence in history.

To run up against the organization is to risk obliteration. In a totalitarian regime, nothing remains after one runs afoul of the organization. Before his arrest, Winston Smith's job was to alter the historical record so as to make it appear that dissidents had never been born. In a democratic society, the sacrificed individual remains. If we listen to him or her we may learn something not just about individuality but about the forces that confront it.

In chapter 6, I define this organization I keep talking about, but not until then. I want first to establish the perspective of the last man, so that we might finally view the organization from his or her perspective (the last man is also a woman). From the perspective of the whistleblower, the organization remains in many ways a feudal entity. Instead of dismissing this perspective as that of the fellow who just got fired by his boss, I suggest we take it seriously – but only after establishing who this last man is and why he or she is so endangered.

How can one best learn from the last man? The answer depends in good measure on what lesson our teacher has to teach. I think the whistleblower has as much to teach us about politics as about suffering. Or rather, it is the suffering of the whistleblower that connects these two terms. The story of the first scapegoat will tell us why. Part of the ancient ritual among the Hebrews for the Day of Atonement, the instructions for the sacrifice of the scapegoat are found in Leviticus 16:21–22: "The priest shall lay both his hands on [the scapegoat] and confess over it all the iniquities of the Israelites and all their acts of rebellion, that is, all their sins; he shall lay them on the head of the she goat and send it away into the wilderness in charge of a man who is waiting ready. The goat shall carry all their iniquities upon itself into some barren waste and the man shall let it go, there in the wilderness."

Think about how much the scapegoat must know. For many whistleblowers this knowledge is like a mortal illness. They live with it, and it with them, every day and night of their lives. They do not just know the sins of the tribe. They are afflicted with them. My plan has been to follow the scapegoat into the desert of his exile and there to study his affliction so that I might learn the sins of the tribe.

You might reply that not only is this way of putting it melodramatic, but how much I can learn depends on how articulate and thoughtful the whistleblower is. About the first objection you will have to decide for yourself. About the second, there are ways of listening that do not depend on the articulateness of the whistleblower. Not everyone is creative, but everyone has a creative unconscious. Not every whistleblower is articulate, but there is eloquence even in silence and cliché if we are prepared to feel its sources. To put the same point another way, I learned most from those whistleblowers who seemed to feel their experiences most deeply, whether or not they were able to articulate them.

When I listen to whistleblowers, I feel awe at one who has stepped outside the skin of the world and lived to tell about it. The whistleblower has become sacred, a term whose original meaning was both blessed and cursed. Daniel Ellsberg, the whistleblower who leaked the Pentagon Papers, said that his former friends and colleagues regarded him with neither admiration nor censure but with wonder, as though he were a space-walking astronaut who had cut his lifeline to the mother ship. What was this mother ship? Was it the academic-military-industrial complex, the system, the organization? Call it what you will, it is not so much a precise concept as an overwhelming feeling.

Every chapter aims to explain this feeling. Every chapter is written from the perspective of this feeling. This is not because the feeling is so important in itself but because of what it tells us about the forces that hold society together and their consequences: the willingness of most people to do anything not to be sent space-walking.

The feeling of space-walking, which is approached in several different ways in the chapters that follow, is best characterized by its opposite – what it means to belong to the organization. What it means, says Edward Shils (1975, 266), is that the organization becomes sacred, so that an instruction from a superior

> is conceived as a "part" or an emanation of the cosmos of commands and judgments at the center of which is the supremely authoritative principle or a supremely authoritative role incorporating that principle. The particular incumbent of the role ... is perceived as the manifestation of a larger center of tremendous power. What the "subject" responds to is not just the specific declaration or order of the incumbent of the role ... but the incumbent enveloped in the vague and powerful nimbus of the authority of the entire institution. It is legitimacy constituted by sharing in the properties of the organization as a whole epitomized or symbolized in the powers concentrated at the peak.

To be a whistleblower is to step outside the Great Chain of Being, to join not just another religion, but another world. Sometimes this other world is called the margins of society, but to the whistleblower it feels like outer space. My theory of whistleblowing, if that is what it is, is no more than a standpoint from which to raise a question. What does the organization look like from the perspective of someone who has been forcibly relocated to this other world?

In order for society to be integrated, says Shils, it must "not only give the impression of being coherent and continuous; it must also appear to be integrated with a transcendent moral order" (1975, 266). Though it sounds dramatic, I argue that being a whistleblower means stepping outside this order. It is a momentous step. Most people, including the whistleblower, don't recognize it as such until the whistleblower has done it. Then he or she knows what it is to go space-walking.

In response, one might argue that Shils is talking about traditional societies. Modern society is marked by multiple centers of meaning, so that, for example, a whistleblower might turn to his or her religion to find meaning after being fired from General Motors for blowing the whistle. It's a good theory, but it does not work so well in real life. Meaning tends to follow power, and power works to discipline the whistleblower in ways that isolate him or her from alternative sources of meaning. Much may be learned by studying how this happens.

6

THIS IS NOT YOUR ORDINARY BOOK ON WHISTLEBLOWERS

Like most books on whistleblowers, there are lots of whistleblower stories here. There the similarity ends. Unlike the authors of most books on whistleblowers, I pay lots of attention to the narrative structure of the whistleblowers' stories. I do this because the stories are fascinating, and their structure helps me understand the stories better. But that is not the main reason. The main reason is that understanding the structure of whistleblowers' stories has helped me develop a theory of ethics and politics based on their experience. This is my goal, and from this goal stems the tension in the manuscript between my desire to tell the whistleblower's story exactly as he or she would wish it to be told, and my desire to tell it in such a way that it illustrates the theory I have developed. I want what is impossible, or at least unfair: to be loyal to whistleblowers' stories only insofar as they illustrate general theories, especially my theory.[1]

The subject wants his or her story told to the world. From the subject's perspective, my job is to tell that story as clearly and interestingly as possible, so that others might know, and so the subject might find in the telling a meaning and order to his or her life. I, in contrast, am interested in finding the sources of disorder in the subject's life, the conflict of voices, so I can formulate a hypothesis about it. Sometimes, the subject will tell me later, this hypothesis was helpful, bringing insight and order. At other times, the subject feels penetrated and misused.

Earlier I said that mine is an account of whistleblower narratives. It is not, however, a recounting. This may disappoint some readers, who expect to encounter the rich and pithy voice of the whistleblower on every page. Though the voice of the whistleblower frequently appears, more in earlier than later chapters, mine is a theory about organizations constructed from the broken narratives of the whistleblower. Mine is not another story told by whistleblowers. I value such stories, I could not have written my book without them, but I do not intend to add to that large literature. My work uses these narratives, conveying enough of their content to share them with the reader, so as to know something about organizational life that is not apparent from the usual top-down perspective.

The stories I tell are concerned with why whistleblowers often have so much trouble being loyal to their story, as Isak Dinesen puts it. For the whistleblower to be loyal to his or her story, he or she would have to know and accept some terrible truths about the world, above all that his sacrifice will not be redeemed. No one will be saved by his suffering, not even himself. The organization he worked for will not be made better, and those who worked with him will not have become more moral by virtue of his example.

How much we can learn depends on how much we are willing to give up. For some whistleblowers it is easier to be disloyal to themselves and their story than to give up all that these truths require. My ethical and political theory concerns what whistleblowers would have to give up to know these truths. Or rather, my theory is inspired by what I think whistleblowers would have to give up to know what they have already learned.

I have said that the whistleblower has difficulty remaining loyal to his or her story. Does this mean that I am loyal to the whistleblower's story, even more loyal than the whistleblower? Not really, at least not in the sense that every whistleblower would agree that I have fully and faithfully represented his or her experience. I am, I believe, loyal to what lies behind the whistleblower's inability to be loyal to his or her story, the dread of giving up the truths of common narrative, that mixture of half-truths, lies, and clichés we tell ourselves about why the world is just and good, or at least good enough to believe in. I hope mine is a higher loyalty, but I cannot be sure.

In trying to think more thoroughly about loyalty, I turned for inspiration to Amazon.com, the on-line bookseller. I found 250 books on loyalty. More than 200 were about keeping consumers and employees loyal. "Brand loyalty" was by far the most frequent use of the term. About 20 books were about "loyalty oaths" during the McCarthy era. Several other were concerned with "my loyalty is my honor," the slogan of Hitler's SS. Only a couple had any relevance to loyalty as a complex moral virtue (Fletcher, 1993).

I think it has become very hard in the United States today to think about loyalty. The term is so old-fashioned that it has become trivialized as "brand loyalty." Or it carries the hint of fascism, as it sometimes should. Even Albert O. Hirschman (1970), in his well-known *Exit, Voice, and Loyalty*, views loyalty strictly as an organizational resource. Loyalty keeps people inside and talking when they would otherwise be leaving. As a result, the organization has a better chance to survive. Whether it should survive is, of course, another question, one Hirschman does not address. Could more terrible things in this world have been done under the banner of loyalty than any other?

In the course of my research, I spoke with a high-level government bureaucrat charged with dealing with whistleblowers. "We have," he said, "fractured and divided government as it is. That's the way the Constitution made it. Look at McNamara and Bundy. They knew the [Vietnam] war was lost, but they didn't speak out. They stayed loyal to Johnson. If we didn't have loyalty, nothing would get done in this government."

"You know," I replied. "The question of effective government is real, and loyalty is a virtue. But when someone mentions loyalty like this I always find myself thinking about the Nazis, and your example doesn't do anything to dissuade me."

Had I not mentioned the Nazis, we might have had a decent conversation, but though he only raised his eyebrows at the time, the bureaucrat had apparently taken offense at this comparison. Just a few minutes later he terminated the interview, but the question remains. Not whether it is fair to compare every organization to Nazis, for of course it is not. Most of all, it matters what we do, and most organizations do not commit atrocities. But this does not mean that the comparison is irrelevant. It just depends on what we are comparing.

Tom Dix, an attorney at the Justice Department, told about coming under increasing pressure from White House lawyers to make his legal opinions conform to their political agenda. Most of his fellow attorneys didn't like it any more than he did, but they stalled and hesitated and eventually went along. Political ideology was not the key issue. Liberal, conservative, or moderate, few of the attorneys liked being the subject of what was in fact illegal political pressure. Eventually Dix went to the staff member of a congressman who sat on an oversight committee. When word leaked back to his boss, all hell broke loose, and it hasn't stopped. He was suspended and has had a lot of time to think about his situation. Dix said: "I keep wondering what my colleagues would have done in 1930s Germany. I wouldn't want to bet that they wouldn't give the Nazis the opinions they wanted. Sure, they'd think the Nazis were trailer trash, and they'd hope the Nazis would be replaced in the next election. But they'd give them the opinions they wanted."

I believe Tom Dix is right, and on this belief much depends. Dix is comparing the ordinary men and women who work at the Justice Department with the ordinary men and women in the justice bureaucracy in Nazi Germany. While separated by half a century and a whole political culture, Dix suspects that these two groups of lawyers are more alike than different, each providing their masters what they want. I suspect the same, but of course I cannot prove it. What I can prove is something about the terrible costs of going up against the organization, costs most of us are not even aware of because they are not apparent until one crosses an invisible line.

AN ETHICS CONFERENCE

In the midst of listening to whistleblowers, I went to an ethics conference. There was a lot of talk about character education, values education, and all the rest but not one word about consequences or costs. All the action was between you and your conscience. It was very Platonic really, desire the enemy of *ethos*, the Greek word for character that comes down to us as ethics. Has the theory and practice of ethics become as idealistic as this in this most materialistic of countries? Or is this a way of making sure that ethics does not get in the way of the real business of making a living?

Contrast the assumption of the participants at the conference with the situation of the whistleblower whose story begins this chapter. His boss asked him to lie to federal investigators, he didn't, and he was fired. His boss prospered, and nothing at the agency has changed. The whistleblower now has trouble making ends meet. He is separated from his wife and alienated from his kids, whom he rarely sees. "My wife just thinks I was a fool. My son and daughter, they think I was selfish, that I didn't think enough of them to put up with what I was asked to do. Maybe they're right. I know my wife is."

Scenarios like this rarely come up in ethics conferences. It is as though ethics were not about power and politics and who pays. At ethics conferences the struggle is located deep in the heart of the human being, the struggle between desire and conscience. Or the scenario is extreme, such as "Would you tell a lie to a Nazi looking for a Jew who was hiding in your basement?" The result of both approaches is not merely to downplay a consideration of consequences but to make ethics separate from politics: the power to make some people pay for others' injustice – that is, the power to make scapegoats.

To be sure, the question of whether you would risk your life to hide a Jew is hardly a question without consequence. But most of us will not be asked to put our lives and the lives of our families on the line for our beliefs. We will more likely be placed in a position of being asked to risk our livelihoods, our way of life. We may be asked, in other words, to take on the role of the scapegoat. Not very much in the conventional discussion of ethics is very helpful in preparing people for this decision, including the question of whether to accept the role in the first place.

The title of the conference I attended was "Ethics in a Diverse Society." No doubt diversity is a valuable goal, making ours a richer and more interesting, as well as more just, society. Diversity is important, but it does not solve the problem considered here, the relationship between the individual and the group.

Diversity means including representatives of previously excluded groups in the organizations that wield power and influence in our society. Treating members of previously excluded groups just like everyone else in the organization is not likely to be helpful when the problem is the inability of the organization to tolerate autonomous individuality in the first place. If everyone's individuality is a resource to be sacrificed in the name of the group, adding more and diverse people to the sacrificial pool is not unambiguously good.

The motto of the school of business where the conference was held was "Capitalizing on the diversity within our community." To capitalize on diversity means to exploit its resources in the name of the goal of the organization, which is to make money and keep power. Here diversity is the catastrophe of liberation about which Herbert Marcuse (1969) wrote many years ago. If previously excluded groups, such as women, are now free to participate in a system that is organized to deny the individuality of everyone who gets to play, this is hardly unadulterated progress.

Phrases such as "deny the individuality" of the organization's members should, of course, raise red flags for the attentive reader. While phrases such as this frequently have no content, I hope to show that this one does. Here I can do no more than to define what I mean by individuality. Later I will address the objection, by Michel Foucault and others, that individuality is a Western philosophical idealization, an incredible story.

We understand individuality best if we appreciate the irony of the term. Individuality means indivisible. Nothing could be further from the truth. To be an individual we must divide ourselves from who we are and what we are doing without falling into ironic detachment. We have to be separate enough from ourselves to have someone to talk to but not so separate that the different internal voices can't hear each other. The ambition, says George Kateb (1992, 97), should be to combine introspection with engagement, each acting as a check on the other. By introspection he doesn't mean self-study; he means reflection – thinking about what one is doing. "One becomes individual in the sense that one tries not to be merely social, tries not to be fully at home in one's social world.... If honest, one becomes almost another to oneself" (1992, 167, 252). Individuality is thought in action, an inner dialogue that makes a difference in what one does, as well as who one is.

Individuality means talking with oneself about what one is doing in a spirit serious enough that it may make a difference in what one does. It sounds simple, but it's not. Hannah Arendt, to whom I will frequently refer, calls this inner conversation "thought." Socrates is thought's hero, the man who was always talking about what he was doing, either with others or with himself.[2] If Socrates epitomizes thought, Adolf Eichmann epitomizes thoughtlessness. What makes Eichmann's evil banal, says Arendt (1964, 49), is that he quite literally never thought about what he was doing.

The ability to have a conversation with oneself does not sound like individuality, the reader might reply. It sounds more like a capacity for self-reflection, not the same thing. Perhaps, but in most of the chapters that follow I will be arguing that it is the whistleblower's ability to talk to himself about what he is doing that explains, if anything can, why he blows the whistle. To think and act on the basis of an inner dialogue may not be the whole of individuality, but it is an important part.[3]

Already I must take back the previous statement. What distinguishes the whistleblower is not his ability to talk with himself but his inability not to. This is certainly how most whistleblowers experience their fate. "It was amazing. Here we were dumping poison into the [environment] and nobody wanted to talk about it, as if talking about it would make it real. Well, it was real all right, but we went around pretending it wasn't. I thought I was going crazy, like it wasn't happening. You think I'm some kind of hero 'cause I blew the whistle. The only reason I spoke up is because I didn't want to go crazy. I had to say what we were doing." Unlike his silent colleagues, this whistleblower couldn't help thinking about what they were doing. Many whistleblowers regret this inability to stop talking with themselves, experiencing it more as curse than blessing.

If whistleblowers are so good at talking with themselves, the reader may be wondering, why do they have so much trouble being loyal to the story – that is, telling themselves what they have learned and listening to themselves tell it? Because talking with oneself is not enough. One has to be able to talk with others who understand. Narrative frames and forms experience, but narrative is not enough. Narrative must be supplemented with dialogue, lest it turn in on itself, an endless narrative forever chasing its tale. For most of us, including Socrates, this turning outward requires partners who gently tug us back into the frames and forms of the shared world. Individuality is not a solitary project but a group one, whose medium is culture. Socrates was lucky to have the sons of wealthy gentlemen as his companions. Who does the whistleblower have?

EXPLAINING WHISTLEBLOWING

Have I just now explained whistleblowing in terms of the whistleblower's inability not to talk with himself? I hope not. Let us consider what it means to answer why someone did something, not just anything, but an act that is rare, risky, and good. Contrast my answer (which is not so much an answer as an explication) with several well-known explanations of the behavior of rescuers of the Jews during the Holocaust. Rescuers are not exactly like whistleblowers (in chapter 4, I specify some differences), but the research on rescuers is more advanced than that on whistleblowers and hence more worthy of criticism. The research on whistleblowers appears to be headed in the same direction, which is not necessarily good.[4]

Consider Eva Fogelman's (1994, xvii) invocation of the "innermost core of a person" as the explanation of why rescuers did it. By this term she means that people said things about themselves that seemed to be consistent over time. Even then Fogelman had to assume that her subjects were not creating a false and artificial consistency by emphasizing some things and de-emphasizing others. The "innermost core of a person" is a description of behavior pretending to be more.

Next consider The Altruistic Personality, the most ambitious correlational study of its kind. Rescuers, say Samuel Oliner and Pearl Oliner (1988), acted out of an attitude of "extensivity," born of their youth in families in which discipline was based on love and moral example, not physical punishment. In practice, this means that 32 percent of rescuers and 39 percent of bystanders (those who saw but did not rescue) received physical punishment. Though rescuers were twice as likely to mention parents' values, 56 percent did not, a majority. Seventy-eight percent of rescuers had supportive and close parental homes, compared with 55 percent (still a majority) of nonrescuers.

These are among the strongest distinctions, no better and generally weaker than those that led Stanley Milgram (1974, 205) to wonder at the weakness of his correlations in his famous study Obedience to Authority. Ordering "teachers" to deliver what they believed were painful electrical shocks to learners, Milgram found no convincing social psychological correlations with disobedience, not even teachers' scores on Lawrence Kohlberg's (1976) famous test of stages of moral development.

Zygmunt Bauman argues that the unpredictability of the rescuer is precisely the point. It is not merely accidental, or a temporary failure of social science, that the rescuer could not be predicted from the usual social scientific categories (sadly, not even previous friendships with Jews). If the rescuer could have been predicted, that would mean that the rescuer fit into the usual categories, which would mean that he or she would not have been a rescuer. The rescuer was the odd man or woman out, the one who didn't fit any of the standard social scientific categories by which human beings are classified. "They came from all corners and sectors of 'social structure,' thereby calling the bluff of there being 'social determinants' of moral behavior. If anything, the contribution of such determinants expressed itself in their failure to extinguish the rescuers' urge to help others in their distress" (Bauman 1989, 5).

If they had been more fully socialized, more average members of their class, religion, educational cohort, and the like, they would not have been rescuers. It is true, of course, but it is not the whole story. Bauman may be read as suggesting that the acts of ethical resisters, such as rescuers and whistleblowers, are in principle inexplicable. That is *not* my argument.

According to Oliner and Oliner (1988, 1–2), who cite the research of Yad Veshem, around fifty thousand non-Jews risked their lives to help Jews survive, out of a European population of several hundred million. Whistleblowers are not as rare as rescuers, but they are not thick on the ground either. The reason rescuers and whistleblowers do it is not likely to be captured by vague and general categories shared by millions, such as "religiosity," "parents' values," and "mode of discipline." Such categories are simply too crude to capture the subtle distinctions necessary. When the behavior in question is unusual, indeed almost vanishingly rare in the case of rescuers and whistleblowers, the usual social psychological categories are insufficiently precise to support a distinction.[5]

This does not mean that the acts of rescuers are inexplicable in terms of categories such as religiosity. It may be that rescuers hold and internalize their religion in different and subtle ways. If one spent hours interviewing each rescuer and bystander about his or her spiritual beliefs (or rather, if one had several interviewers spend hours separately interviewing them so as to control for interviewer subjectivity), one might be able to get at the difference and perhaps even put it into numbers. But neither Oliner and Oliner nor anyone else has even come close to combining breadth and depth of analysis in this way. No one has come close in the study of whistleblowers either.[6]

Milgram makes a similar argument. Not that there is no way to know how those who obeyed authority differed from those who did not, but the available paper and pencil psychological tests, including Kohlberg's, are insufficiently subtle to pick up the difference.

Explanations are more phenomenological than we know. Thinking we are explaining the sources and causes of something (even when we are careful to call it an "association"), we often do little more than describe the phenomenon in other words.[7] Explaining the actions of whistleblowers or rescuers is not so much about distinguishing them from bystanders as it is understanding how whistleblowers and rescuers experienced their world by listening to the stories they tell about it.

CHAPTER 2

Don't Just Do It to Save Lives

They wouldn't talk with me about what I said, and they wouldn't talk with me about not talking about it. – A whistleblower

BEFORE continuing, it may be helpful to define the whistle-blower I am talking about. A common definition, that of Myron Glazer and Penina Glazer (1989, 4) in *The Whistleblowers*, defines the whistleblower as one who (1) acts to prevent harm to others, not him or herself, (2) trying first to rectify the situation within the framework provided by the organization, (3) while possessing evidence that would convince a reasonable person. The harm may be physical, such as the illegal disposal of toxic waste; financial, such as the waste or misuse of taxpayers' money; or legal, the breaking of laws. Often it is all three.

Part 2 of Glazer and Glazer's definition cannot possibly be considered a definition, only a piece of advice. Daniel Ellsberg is no less a whistleblower because he did not first go to the chairman of the Joint Chiefs of Staff and ask to release the Pentagon Papers. Neither is part 3 of the definition very useful, though it must be admitted that the law is filled with reasonable men and their standards.

Inserted, presumably, to distinguish whistleblower fantasy from intersubjectively shared reality, the reasonable person actually represents the citizen for whom the whistleblower speaks. If the citizen heard both sides, would he find the whistleblower's complaint plausible? Putting it this way might generate a rational standard, but it does not seem a necessary part of the definition itself. An unreasonable whistleblower is still a whistleblower. Like so many, Glazer and Glazer are evidently afraid of the stereotype of the whistleblower as hysterical malcontent, eliminating the possibility in advance by definition. In any case, the key point is the first one.

It is admirable, but it is not whistleblowing, to complain of sexual harassment or racial prejudice against oneself.[1] In addition, most would not consider it whistleblowing to complain of an act of sexual harassment against a colleague unless this harassment was part of a pattern that was ignored by management.

Some would restrict whistleblowing to issues in which an overriding societal value is at stake, such as health, safety, or fiduciary duty. "Do it to save lives, or don't do it," a policy suggested by one whistleblower, expresses this restriction in its strongest form. But terms like "overriding" may cause more trouble than they are worth, except insofar as they suggest that stupid decisions are not the same as unethical ones.

In theory, anyone who speaks out in the name of the public good within the organization is a whistleblower. In practice, the whistleblower is defined by the retaliation he or she receives. Imagine that an employee observes an unethical or illegal act by her boss and reports it to her boss's boss. This is the situation that is most likely to get the employee into trouble. Rarely do employees get fired for reporting the misbehavior of subordinates.

Her boss's boss thanks her for the information and corrects the problem. She has performed an act of whistleblowing, but for all practical purposes she is not a whistleblower. She becomes a whistleblower only when she experiences retaliation. If there is no retaliation, she is just a responsible employee doing her job to protect the company's interest. This probably results in overstating the amount of retaliation against whistleblowers. If the whistleblower is defined by the organization's response, then by definition most whistleblowers are retaliated against, and most of them severely.

Somewhere between half and two-thirds of the whistleblowers lose their jobs, according to several studies (Miethe 1999, 77–78; Rothschild and Miethe 1996, 15–16; Glazer and Glazer 1989, 206–7). At least one study, however, has found significantly less retaliation (Miceli and Near 1992, 226–27). As might be expected, most of the difference depends on whom and how one counts (Miethe 1999, 73–78).

Though I approach whistleblowing differently from the studies to which I refer, the characteristics of the small group of whistleblowers I worked with fit the statistical profile of the average whistleblower in the literature remarkably closely.[2] I did not intend to find this resemblance. I did not seek whistleblowers who fit the profile, just whistleblowers who would talk about their experiences.

Among the whistleblowers I worked with, a little over two-thirds lost their jobs. I found most (but far from all) of the whistleblowers I interviewed through a support and lobbying group for whistleblowers, which may have attracted those who had been punished most severely. The whistleblowers in the group were more likely to be employed by government agencies, however, and it is harder for government than private industry to fire someone for whistleblowing.

Seniority and rank offer little protection, as several studies reveal (Devine 1998). On the contrary, many organizations seem most threatened by what they view as defection within the senior ranks and hence are most willing to make an example of the defector. The biggest variable is whether the wrongdoing involved losses to the organization of more than $100,000 and whether the reported conduct was routine. If the answer to both these questions was yes, the whistleblower was most likely to be fired (Rothschild and Miethe 1996, 17). The more systematic the wrongdoing, the greater the reprisal (Miethe 1999, 81).

Not only do most whistleblowers get fired, but they rarely get their jobs back. Most never work in the field again. In some tight-knit fields there is an informal blacklist. One whistleblower was fired from her new job in the pharmaceutical industry when she sued a previous employer for wrongful discharge. "[My new boss] said it was unconscionable that anyone working for Personal Products would sue a sister company." (Glazer and Glazer 1989, 95) When all organizations are sisters, the whistleblower has nowhere else to go. That, presumably, is the point.

Of the several dozen whistleblowers I have talked with, most lost their houses. Many lost their families. It doesn't happen all at once, but whistleblowers' cases drag on for years, putting a tremendous strain on families. Most whistleblowers will suffer from depression and alcoholism (Clark 1997, 1065; Miethe 1999, 77–78). Miethe (1999, 78) found that half went bankrupt. Most whistleblowers will be unable to retire. A typical fate is for a nuclear engineer to end up selling computers at Radio Shack.

These are tremendous shocks to the whistleblower. They are not, I believe, the greatest shock. The greatest shock is what the whistleblower learns about the world as a result – that nothing he or she believed was true. That people can be so deeply shaken by knowledge is not something I had expected to find.

One surprising result of these empirical studies of whistleblowing deserves further consideration. One would think that it would make a big difference as to whether retaliation occurred if the whistleblower went first to the newspapers or to the boss. In fact, it makes surprisingly little difference. Miethe (1999, 80) found that it makes only a 10-percent difference. Why would internal whistleblowing, as it is called, be so threatening to the organization that its consequences are virtually the same as for external whistleblowing? People lose not only their jobs but in many cases their careers.[3]

In creating the whistleblower, the organization is stating that there is a certain type of person it cannot stand in its midst, not necessarily one who goes outside the organization but one who appears to remember that there is an outside. One whistleblower put it this way: "I decided I needed to go back to work. I interviewed with the state of Texas, the city of Austin, and many industries. . . . But nobody wants to hire former whistleblowers. They are all afraid of what we would do if we were asked to tell the truth about some problem" (Glazer and Glazer 1989, 228).

In chapter 1, I defined individuality as the ability to carry on an internal dialogue with oneself about what one is doing, a dialogue authentic enough that it might result in doing something different. I have not yet defined the organization I keep talking about and will not until chapter 6, where its definition will be the leading topic. The key point for now is that whistleblowing is not just an act of speaking out. It is an assertion of individuality, perhaps a more basic assertion, in which we talk with others about what we are doing as we are doing it.

It turns out to be surprisingly difficult for whistleblowers to share their internal dialogue with others in the organization. Not only does no one want to listen, but no one wants to talk about not listening. A common comment was the following: "I said I'd do anything [the boss] wanted – keep silent, resign, ask for a transfer. All he had to do was discuss the issue with me. But he wouldn't do it, and he wouldn't talk about not doing it. My insubordination was the only issue."

We don't know how important being subordinate is, we don't properly estimate the borders of subservience, until we cross them. Engaging in ethical discourse within the organization is one way to learn these limits quickly, but only in retrospect. At the time there is something crazy-making about the experience, akin to the double bind that was once said to cause schizophrenia. Don't talk about ethical issues, and don't talk about our not talking about ethical issues. In the first case recounted below, Peter James Atherton's supervisors refused to read his report; they would not even allow it to be typed. When it finally emerged, almost two decades later, it was his handwritten version that had been preserved in a little library in Maine.

Below are stories of four who spoke out and one who did not but should have. In each story not only would the organization not listen, but it transformed issues of ethics, politics, and policy into a single question, that of insubordination. There is a reason for this. Bauman (1989, 213–15) puts it trenchantly. All social organization, he says,

> consists in subjecting the conduct of its units to either instrumental or procedural criteria of evaluation. More importantly still, it consists in delegalizing all other criteria, and first and foremost such standards as may render behaviour of units resilient to uniformizing pressures and thus autonomous vis-à-vis the collective purpose of the organization (which, from the organizational point of view, makes them unpredictable and potentially de-stabilizing).... All social organization consists therefore in neutralizing the disruptive and deregulating impact of moral behavior.[4]

The best way to disrupt moral behavior is not to discuss it and not to discuss not discussing it. Then it doesn't exist. Right?

When I say that the organization quells individuality, this is what I mean. Talking about what we are doing is not just talking about process and procedures, how we are going to do it. Talking about what we are doing means talking about how what we do affects others. Talking about what we are doing puts our actions in the larger context of their influence on a world of others. Talking about what we are doing makes these others present, as though they were represented in the discussion. Jürgen Habermas (1984) makes this the mark of communicative rationality, the rationality of the lifeworld, as opposed to the rationality of science and technology, what Bauman calls instrumental or procedural criteria of evaluation.

Mine is not a "should" statement; it is an "is" statement. I am not arguing that the organization should care about others outside the organization, only that talking about what one is doing *means* talking about the effects of one's acts on those outside the organization and whether these effects are good or bad, right or wrong.

We live in a moral world, not because people are good, or because people always think morally about what they are doing, but because as human beings the categories of right and wrong are part of our natural moral environment.[5] To talk about what one is doing is, in part, to raise these considerations, to make explicit the moral context that is always implicit. To talk about what one is doing means to engage in what Hannah Arendt calls thought, and that is no small deed. For the organizations where these whistleblowers worked, it was too much.

ATHERTON AND THE NRC

Peter James Atherton is his name, one of the few actual names of whistleblowers used in this book. I use it because he asked me to and because his case is well known. His is not a typical story, but it illustrates much that is. A nuclear engineer and inspector for the Nuclear Regulatory Commission, Atherton became convinced that the electrical cables that would be needed to shut down the Maine Yankee nuclear plant in an emergency were not properly separated. If one failed because of fire, all would fail because they were routed through the same cable tray, as it is called. The plant should be shut down until this and other deficiencies were corrected.

Atherton's concerns were not based on fantasy. Just three years earlier, in 1975, some workers used a candle flame to check for air leaks in the containment building that housed the reactor at the

Brown's Ferry nuclear plant. The flame touched some insulation, igniting a fire that burned more than two thousand cables and disabled electrical controls at the plant. It took more than three days to shut down the plant's two operating reactors, one of which came close to boiling off its cooling water. Had that happened, a meltdown would have occurred.

In the keep 'em glowing climate of the 1970s, plants were rarely shut down for repairs. Atherton's supervisors were aware of his conclusions, and while he was preparing his report they began preparing a response. Their position was that Atherton was emotionally ill, his report an exaggeration. The NRC would not type up his report, and Atherton began showing a handwritten copy to his colleagues. They refused to read it, and so did his supervisors, or so they said.[6]

On the day the NRC met with Maine Yankee officials, Atherton got in his car, drove to downtown Washington, D.C., and carried his report straight to NRC commissioner Victor Gilinsky. When Gilinsky would not shut down Maine Yankee immediately, Atherton went to the top nuclear engineer in the country, President Jimmy Carter. After showing his NRC credentials to the Secret Service agent at the gate, he was admitted to the White House grounds, handcuffed, and sent to St. Elizabeth's Hospital for three days of involuntary psychiatric confinement. He was released and fired.

Atherton is in many ways the consummate outsider. Twenty years later he lives in a third-floor room in an aging apartment building in Washington, his room as spartan as a monk's. He sleeps on a mattress on box springs, pulling out a folding metal chair for his guest. Instead of paying rent, he does odd jobs for the owner. He is said to have lived out of his car for a while, but to me he denies it.[7]

Although he looks and acts the part of the outsider, the anti-organization man, the anarchic individualist in a corporate world, he did not behave that way on the job. On the contrary, he is proud that he stayed within the chain of command, never going outside. "Jimmy Carter was in the nuclear navy. He was my boss. I never went outside the chain of command, not once. No one ever appreciated that."

No one ever will. Atherton is threatening not because he threatened to go outside but because he represents the presence of the outside on the inside: not just the unassimilated individual but the unassimilated citizen. Atherton did not "go public." He spoke for the public in private, bringing the outer world into the inner, transgressing boundaries.

Atherton is unassimilated to organizational culture, above all to the idea that one formulates one's position not in response to one's analysis of the situation outside but in response to the situation inside: the expectations of one's superiors, the organizational lay of the land. There are no naive empiricists and positivists in organizational life. Or if there are, they do not last long. One study of whistleblowers found them among the least sensitive to social cues (Jos, Tompkins, and Hays 1989).

A Postscript

In 1991, a short-circuit set off a hydrogen gas explosion in the turbine building of the Maine Yankee plant. Supporting beams were bent, and bolts were sheared, splitting pipes that carried hydrogen gas to the plant's generator. Hydrogen fires burned for hours. The plant was shut down for repairs, and anti-nuclear activists in Maine were reinvigorated. One activist found a copy of Atherton's handwritten report in the public documents room in a local library. In addition to the cable separation problem, it described a hydrogen explosion hazard almost identical to the one that had just occurred. No one, including Atherton, knows how his report ended up in a little library in Maine. The local paper, the *Lincoln County Weekly*, wrote a story headlined "NRC Knew of Problems 20 Years Ago." Still in question was whether the cables that Atherton cited were the same ones that short-circuited.

After an investigation lasting several years, the NRC found additional problems. "The most prevalent one was insufficient separation of safety cables and other wires. Some wires were so close together they might short out" (Weisman 1997). In December 1996, Maine Yankee shut the plant down, pending repair of the separation problem, the same problem Atherton identified nearly twenty years earlier.

Maine Yankee has decided that repairs cost too much and has closed the plant for good. The NRC has launched two investigations into the Atherton matter, one on the technical issues he identified, the other by the inspector general on the circumstances of his dismissal.

The investigations continue. It is not unusual for a whistleblower's case to drag on this long, now more than twenty years.

When I asked Atherton what he thought about the story about him in the *Washington Post Magazine* that laid his personal life bare, he said he spoke to the reporter honestly about his trials in the hope that it might interest him enough to write something about his case. Atherton means the technical details, fire hazards and cable separation. He has learned about using the media, but strictly in the service of his cause. For all his passion, he is strangely distant from his story. Coupled with his black and gray beard, it is what gives him the quality of an Old Testament prophet transported by his cause.

Atherton will in all likelihood never get his job back. It is unlikely that he will be compensated in any way for his twenty years in the desert. Yet he has received something that few whistleblowers do, a sort of public vindication. It is what almost every whistleblower seeks. When it comes (and it is rare), it helps, but not as much as one might suppose, certainly not as much as the whistleblower had hoped. He has learned and gone through too much.

ROBERT HARRIS AND THE DEPARTMENT OF DEFENSE

Robert Harris was a major in the United States Army before his retirement, when he became the chief procurement officer for a Defense Department installation. He continued working for the army but as a civilian. Within two years of assuming his new job he won the secretary of the army's Award for Outstanding Achievement in Acquisitions. Like many whistleblowers, he is a patriotic, conservative, middle-aged man who identified with the system. His father was a general, and he still believes that "an officer's word is his bond," what he calls the Old Army tradition. "I wasn't looking to make trouble. I had two kids in college, and I just wanted to see them on their own before I left the workforce."

Several years into his job he was asked to write a purchase order for a sole source contract. Evidently some army colleagues had retired about the same time as he, going to work for the consulting firm that recommended awarding a sole source contract to Armscomp, a manufacturer of specialized computing equipment.

I asked Harris if he thought the consultants were getting kickbacks from Armscomp. "Maybe, maybe not," Harris replied. "There wasn't a lot of money involved. Ten million, but for the army that's peanuts. [The consultants] might have just been trying to help their buddies who founded Armscomp. [The consultants] were way out of their field of their expertise. They wanted their $30,000 a week as quick and easy as possible."

Harris convinced his commander not to issue the contract and instead to issue a solicitation for competitive bids. Less than a week later the competition was halted by a telephone call from a general in the Pentagon, who said that if the contract was not let as originally written, the installation might not have enough work to justify the next year's budget. Harris is certain that the consultants, all former officers, got a friendly senior officer at the Pentagon to make the call to his commander. Harris's commander quickly canceled the solicitation but made no move against him, congratulating him on his "due diligence," and telling him it was time to drop the matter.

Harris didn't drop it. When the officer who canceled the solicitation ignored his faxes, Harris wrote the secretary of the army, contacted the inspector general, and finally reached Senator David Pryor, whose congressional committee was investigating procurement fraud. A two-year investigation followed, but it was dropped when the Republicans won the 1994 election and Pryor lost his chairmanship of the Senate Governmental Affairs Subcommittee. Eventually the inspector general found the contract award improper, but not illegal. But the computers had already been delivered, and there was little else the inspector general could do. Army investigators found that no criminal bribes had been taken.

Harris's days at his job were numbered. He was given an evening shift, then transferred to a job sixty miles away, where he was told he could not use the telephone or fax. Soon he was denied access to the copier. His computer was confiscated. A series of bad efficiency reports followed. In a little less than two years he was fired.

Harris's story is typical. Matters of life and death were not involved. He was given an opportunity to back off but did not. That Harris was not immediately fired is also typical. Instead, he was put through a series of trials designed to enrage and humiliate him or perhaps simply to ensure that he could not perform his job. When his inability to perform properly had been documented in several consecutive efficiency reports, he was fired. The record showed no connection between his blowing the whistle and his termination.

Also typical is his reply to my question, "Why did you blow the whistle?"

"I honestly did not think of my having blown the whistle until the inspector general for the DoD audit team started telling me about the Whistleblower Protection Act. I was paid to use my skill and intellect to protect the taxpayers' purse. I was just doing my job. . . . I was absolutely ecstatic when I first convinced the [military installation] commander to compete for bids. When the assistant inspector general for auditing personally called and said he'd take my case, I was sure that it was all over, that my part was done. I didn't realize the brass was just waiting for the IG to finish his report before they retaliated."

Harris continues to contact newspapers and to speak with anyone who will listen. He has established several web sites that tell his story in excruciating detail. One contains the following statement:

> A whistleblower on government contract fraud is most akin to the tree
> that falls in the forest trapping an animal of nature with no one around
> – the falling actually occurred and the animal dies, but no one listened,
> no one helped the animal, and the cycle continues.

Still, Harris continues to tell his story. He seems convinced that if he can just find the right words to tell it, someone with the power to set things right will listen. It is a common delusion among whistleblowers.

THOMAS HARDY AND THE STATE DEPARTMENT

Hardy served in several foreign posts for the United States government before joining the Foreign Service in mid-career. After a two-year posting in France, he was assigned to the United States embassy in a Middle Eastern country. The U.S. consulate there made abundant provisions for Islamic worship but refused to provide similar accommodations for Christians. Although officials allowed a small group of Catholics to meet surreptitiously (their service was called the "Tuesday Lecture"),

Hardy says he was told to deny that the practice existed if any newcomers wished to join. Protestants and Mormons were denied any opportunity for public worship on the embassy grounds. Since Christian worship was illegal throughout the land, this rule prevented them from practicing their religion in public. Jewish diplomats were not knowingly assigned to the post. All these practices were defended as necessary to prevent security threats to the embassy, evidently from outraged Islamic extremists.

Hardy protested these restrictions on freedom of religion on what was technically, he says, U.S. sovereign territory. He believes the United States Constitution was being violated. When he protested to his superiors, he was warned to drop the issue lest the Catholic services be discontinued as well. When he told visiting officials from the inspector general's office of his concern, he was ordered to return to the United States. There he was required to take psychological tests and eventually was fired.

A United States congressman who has supported Hardy noted in the *Congressional Record* that he was fired just seventy-three days before he would have been vested in the Foreign Service retirement plan. A review panel at the State Department, established after the intervention of several congressmen, explained that Hardy had not "absorbed the foreign service culture." Since then, Hardy's case has been taken up by half a dozen religious groups. Sympathetic accounts of his case have run in the *Wall Street Journal*, *Human Events*, and the *American Spectator*.

Hardy has since appealed the department's action, lodged a complaint with the U.S. Commission on Civil Rights, and filed suit in federal court. Several years have passed, and his appeals are all still pending. He was unemployed for several years, during which he lost his home, filed for bankruptcy, and became seriously ill.

Many people, including myself, wonder if Hardy did the right thing. Did the embassy really have legitimate security concerns? Was this an issue worth losing one's career over? The answer is that it does not matter, just as it does not matter if any particular whistleblower is right or wrong. Opinions will vary on particular cases; reasonable people will disagree. What matters is the way the organization deals with dissent – what happens within the organization when principled dissent becomes impossible. To insist on purity and clarity in every case before one can make a judgment is not so much intellectual responsibility as intellectual timidity, as though one dare not criticize unless the critic is perfect. All that matters is that the whistleblower's case be reasonable, as Hardy's case was. It is all that matters because the task is not to judge the whistleblower but to understand the experience of the scapegoat so that we might learn from him or her about the sins of our tribe.

LAURA BASTION AND THE DEPARTMENT OF DEFENSE

Laura Bastion, a child psychologist, was a civilian working for the Department of Defense in Europe. Her job was to evaluate and treat the "exceptional children" of military personnel. She owed her job to congressional legislation mandating that the disabled children of servicemen and women receive the special education necessary to develop their potential to the fullest.

Soon after her arrival in Europe, Bastion realized that the military was making only a token effort. On a large military base with hundreds of children with special needs, she and another psychologist were overwhelmed. The problem, she said, was not that they were unable to devote sufficient time to each child but that they could not even evaluate most of the children with special needs.

After she had been on the job for a little over a year, a team from the Pentagon that had developed the program for disabled children visited her base to evaluate its implementation. She expressed her concerns to the team members, and they were supportive, asking her to write up a report and send it to them. She thought they seemed excited that she was telling the truth about the situation. They took her to dinner, and she felt that they had the will and the resources to make a change.

Soon her immediate supervisor found out about the report she had filed. At first he too was supportive, saying he shared her concerns. Only when his superiors at the Pentagon began to question his management of the program did he change his tune. Her office was moved to a basement broom closet, and she was sent for psychological evaluation. Soon she was assigned a "handler," as she put it, a new immediate supervisor whose job seemed to be to find pretexts for writing her up, such as an "inappropriate comment" she made regarding a "two for one special" when she came across two children with the same disability in one week. She did not make this comment to the children or their parents, only to a supervisor, but that was enough. A series of bad efficiency reports followed, and she was forced to resign (a "constructive discharge" it is called) within eighteen months. All told she had been in her position less than three years. Her boss has since been promoted. Her handler received an award.

Never, she says, did the team from the Pentagon act to protect her once the retaliation began. She never heard from them again. She called the team leader, and he said he was no longer with that department. Bastion believes that education for disabled children was never a priority with the military but that the intention was only to make a token effort. In other words, it was policy, not faulty implementation, that she interfered with. Her boss was fulfilling the wishes of his superiors to run a token program.

Bastion spent more than $100,000 taking her case through the federal courts. She lost her last appeal. The trial judge ruled that although she had been forced to resign, she was not protected under the rehabilitation act under which she complained. The appellate judge concurred. Unlike many whistleblowers, she has continued to work in her profession.

DUVON MCGUIRE AND THE GENTLEMAN'S AGREEMENT
A newspaper story told of Duvon McGuire, a home insulation specialist, who in 1988 served on a subcommittee of the American Society of Testing and Materials, which established the standards by which the Federal Aviation Administration (FAA) judged the safety of airline insulation. McGuire realized at the time that the method used for testing, holding the material over a Bunsen burner, was "meaningless ... the technological equivalent of running your finger through a candle flame." Almost any material would pass. He fired off a memo to the subcommittee and eventually voted no when the subcommittee met to confirm the standards. Soon, however, he was persuaded to change his vote.[8]

McGuire, now self-employed, said that under a "gentleman's agreement" with the subcommittee, he withdrew his negative vote in exchange for a promise that the subcommittee would revisit the issue, which never happened. McGuire said that he never made any independent effort to contact the FAA, which he now regrets (Phillips 1998).

Since 1988, several hundred people have died in aircraft fires whose spread and intensity have been attributed to the material originally tested by McGuire. Had McGuire been less of a gentleman, lives might have been saved. It is, in the end, the gentleman's agreement that the whistleblower violates, which shows how much the organization depends on such agreements. Or rather, the organization *is* such agreements because the institution is the pattern of social arrangements over time.

THEMES
Several themes that are consistent through these stories will reappear throughout this book.

1. With the exception of Atherton's, none of the whistleblowers' stories are particularly dramatic. I have listened to at least half a dozen whistleblowers whose cases are as startling as Atherton's, but to have included them would miss the point. Whistleblowing is not about the lone individual standing between the organization and the deaths of hundreds, though the case of Duvon McGuire reminds us that such situations exist.

Whistleblowing is about the quirky individual speaking out in a situation of moral ambiguity. Few will ever know his or her fate except those in the organization who are intimidated into even deeper silence by his or her sacrifice. This aspect of organizational life is difficult to know because it is so silent. Whistleblowers provide a glimpse into this aspect. To sacrifice this glimpse for individual drama would be to get it backward. What needs to be known is not the drama of the whistleblower but the drama of everyday organizational life.[9]

2. Usually the whistleblower is not fired outright. The organization's goal is to disconnect the act of whistleblowing from the act of retaliation, which is why so much legislation to protect the whistleblower is practically irrelevant. The usual practice is to demoralize and

humiliate the whistleblower, putting him or her under so much psychological stress that it becomes difficult to do a good job. If the whistleblower is under enough stress, he or she is likely to make a bad decision, justifying disciplinary actions. A surprising number of whistleblowers have been given closets for offices. One was ordered to go into his closet at nine and not come out until five. A few whistleblowers have been transferred to positions for which they lacked the requisite skills, virtually guaranteeing that they would fail. A series of bad efficiency reports would follow, along with psychological evaluations. Only then was the whistleblower dismissed.

It is possible that those who the whistleblower sees as seeking vengeance see themselves as eliminating a disruptive and unsocialized employee whose loyalty cannot be trusted. I am not concerned about motives, only about organizations.

3. The key organizational strategy is to transform an act of whistleblowing from an issue of policy and principle into an act of private disobedience and psychological disturbance. It is the organization's strategy of making the whistleblower the issue that leads me to draw on the work of Michel Foucault in chapter 6. More than any other theorist, Foucault is concerned with the way political disagreement is transformed into private acts that may be subject to discipline. The academic study of whistleblowers should not unwittingly repeat the disciplinary strategy of the organization in the guise of an intellectual strategy that makes whistleblower psychology or the intellectual and ethical purity of the whistleblower's case central.

My question is not, "Was the whistleblower right (pure, just, well-balanced)?" but "What can the whistleblower's experience teach us about the fate of the individual in the organization?" To know this (that is, to be sure that there are not too many disturbances in the field), it is enough that the whistleblower not be crazy and that his or her case not be totally implausible. To demand that genuine whistleblowers be among the most rational, ethical, well-balanced, and humane of humans would obscure most of what is important by making it impossible to ask the right question. Not "Who is the whistleblower and is his case sounder than sound?" but "What can we learn from the experience of the scapegoat?" is the question I am interested in.

4. None of these whistleblowers went directly to the media (none went to the media until after they were fired). Most were protesting in-house, blowing the whistle internally, as it is called. The problem is that for the organization the "house" definitely does not include the inspector general's office and usually not even the boss's boss. In other words, the house is very small, sometimes as small as the boss and his or her subordinates.

5. Most of the whistleblowers I spoke with worked for the government, though many worked in the private sector. Some studies have found significant differences between public and private whistleblowing. Although employees of private organizations seem to observe at least as much corruption as public employees, they are somewhat less likely to report it (Miethe 1999, 39–43). The difference is probably related to do the relative ease with which private employers can terminate whistleblowers. The common law employment-at-will doctrine still permits an employer to dismiss an employee even for a "cause morally wrong" (Elliston et al. 1985b, 100). Law and judicial decisions are creating exceptions to employment-at-will almost daily (Miethe 1999, 95). Enforcing the law staking out these exceptions is another matter.

All in all, the differences between private and public whistleblowing are not substantial, and it is easy to see why. The distinction between public and private is itself blurred. Every employee of every federal contractor is covered by dozens of federal laws protecting whistleblowers. Every employee of every organization regulated by the federal government, from mines to nuclear power plants, is covered by similar legislation. These laws are discussed in chapter 6. Hundreds of laws protect whistleblowers, which means – in effect – that whistleblowers must be gotten rid of in ways that are in accordance with the law. These ways do not vary greatly between the public and private sectors. Some have been demonstrated in the preceding accounts.

"DO IT TO SAVE LIVES OR DON'T DO IT"

At the "Future of Whistleblowing," a conference organized by the Government Accountability Project, a whistleblower advocacy group, every single attorney said he or she advised clients not to blow the whistle but to find another way. It costs too much, and it hurts too much. On a network radio talk show on whistleblowing in 1998, every whistleblower who called in but one said he or she would not do it again.

Most whistleblowers I have spoken with reached the same conclusion: don't do it; the cost is too high. Said Al Ripskis, who kept his job after blowing the whistle on the Environmental Protection Agency's failure to enforce its own rules. "My advice to potential whistleblowers can be summarized in two words: Forget it!"

It will cost you your career and your house and probably drive you into bankruptcy (Glazer and Glazer 1989, 206). It is not a comforting story or an inspiring one. "Federal employees should not have to be martyrs" is how one psychologist who specializes in working with whistleblowers puts it. By the time they get to him most already are.

It is not what we want to hear. It is not what the heroic individual is supposed to say. He or she is supposed to say that "despite all the suffering and hardship, I know I did the right thing, and I would do it again if I had to." One study reports that 90 percent of whistleblowers say this (Rothschild and Miethe 1996, 17). This is not what most whistleblowers said to me.

Nor is it what a whistleblower in the audience at the Future of Whistleblowing conference said. He was, he said, upset at all the "don't do it, it's not worth it" talk. Sometimes you just have to do the right thing. At the same time he knew, from his own experience, what it cost to be a whistleblower. His conclusion was to reach a compromise, the compromise he'd arrived at in his own case. "Do it to save lives," he said. "Do it to save lives, or don't do it." Most in the audience seemed to agree, and there it ended. Don't do it unless it is to save lives; then do it.

It is a terrible compromise, and not just because it is often unclear when lives are at stake and what will save them, as the case of Duvon McGuire illustrates. It is a terrible compromise because it divides the world into heroes and banal bureaucrats, leaving nothing left over for citizens. It is not the acts of heroes that will save the republic. It is the acts of citizens, men and women who remember the public when they are acting in private, which includes government agencies.

A large group of political scientists believe that the leading problem in the United States today is the loss of a sense of community and belonging. Robert Putnam (2000) writes that more Americans are bowling alone – that is, not participating in the low-level civic life of the country, such as belonging to the PTA or a bowling league, groups on which the republic depends. These associations are called civil society. Their absence results in feelings of powerless and anomie, dealt with by strategies of self-aggrandizement – from cosmetic surgery to voting to privatize social security, an oxymoron that no one seems to notice.

The fate of the whistleblower is not the worst problem our society faces, but it illuminates many others. With the whistleblower one sees not just the fate of the individual in mass democracy but the fate of the individual in the organization that is situated in mass democracy. For a long time people have worried about whether the large organization in which most people live their lives contributes to teaching democratic values. Richard Sennett (1998) believes that the values of the contemporary workplace are undermining the values of the rest of our lives. The fate of the whistleblower heightens these issues, showing that not only does the modern organization do little to foster civic values but that it is committed to the destruction of the individual who displays them.

If my argument about whistleblowers is correct, the proponents of civil society are grasping at straws. Organizations are not just undemocratic. Organizations are the enemy of individual morality. Individuals who depend on these organizations for their livelihoods may become democrats in their communities in their off-hours, but there will always be something false and partial about it. Large organizations, private and public alike, don't just control the political agenda. They are the political world that matters most to people's lives, that part of politics that controls your career, your paycheck, your health insurance, your mortgage, your retirement, and your family's economic security. Until there is room for the ethical individual in these organizations – until, that is, there is ethical commerce between the organization and civil society – the associations that make up civil society will have the quality of a hobby. Bowling with other people is better than bowling alone, but it is not real politics either.[10]

Legislation is now being crafted in at least one federal agency to protect the anonymity of whistleblowers in the private sector, requiring both government and company to act on anonymous reports of wrongdoing. Several groups now sponsor whistleblowing without whistleblowers. They forward the complaints of whistleblowers, without identifying characteristics, to the appropriate agencies. Whistleblower.com is one. PEER (Public Employees for Environmental Responsibility) is another. A newspaper article, basically friendly, writes that "PEER offers its members a sort of vanity press, which publishes anonymous 'white papers' railing against Federal and state agencies" (Perlstein 1998).

Anonymous whistleblowing happens when ethical discourse becomes impossible, when acting ethically is tantamount to becoming a scapegoat. It is an instrumental solution to a discursive problem, the problem of not being able to talk about what we are doing. Whistleblowing without whistleblowers is not a future we should aspire to, any more than individuality without individuals or citizenship without citizens. If everyone has to hide in order to say anything of ethical consequence (as opposed to "mere" political opinion), then we will all end our days as drivers on a vast freeway: darkened windshields, darkened license plate holders, dark glasses, speeding aggressively to God knows where.

CHAPTER 3

Whistleblowers' Narratives: Stuck in Static Time

"All sorrows can be borne if you put them into a story or tell a story about them." The story reveals the meaning of what otherwise would remain an unbearable sequence of sheer happenings. – Hannah Arendt, "Isak Dinesen"

I F we consider that the terms "borne" and "born" share a common origin in the term "bear," as in to bear a burden or a child, then the problem of the whistleblower is that he can't give birth to his story. The whistleblower is unable to give her story a narrative frame and form that allows it to be successfully endured. I have written of this problem in terms of the whistleblower's inability to be loyal to his or her story. To do so would require that the whistleblower give up too much. This chapter is about what exactly the whistleblower would have to give up.

But it is not so simple as that. There is something misleading about the image of the lone whistleblower, standing naked to the wind and rain, struggling to give up his last illusion, at which point he will finally be free. The real problem is more prosaic. The whistleblower has only his narrative. He or she also needs someone to talk with, someone who will hear the narrative and so help the whistleblower make it his own. Narrative is best framed and formed as it enters into discourse. In the absence of a discursive frame, narrative tends to turn in on itself, like a snake biting its tail. Without someone to share it with, narrative risks becoming an endless monologue.

Below I recount four prominent themes of whistleblowers' narratives. The narratives of most whistleblowers include the first three themes, less often the fourth. In a long narrative one theme will generally predominate, and it is by its predominant pattern of expression that I have characterized these narratives. The four themes are choice-less choice, stuck in static time, paranoid themes, and "living in the position of the dead." The fourth theme represents, I believe, a re-source for richer narrative forms, as well as richer lives.

My inspiration is Lawrence Langer's *Holocaust Testimonies: The Ruins of Memory* (1991). Langer discovers an almost overwhelming impulse to transform the narratives of survivors into inspirational tales. Most listeners can't or won't hear the shattered meaning that can never be made good, or even meaningful – if, that is, we equate meaningful with whole, coherent, and inspiring, not cold and broken. Whistle-blowers have gone through far, far less, but the principle still applies. The Frankfurt School of Critical Theory made a similar argument about aesthetics: any artistic rendering of the horrible and grotesque must misrepresent it by making it beautiful, in form if not content, for that is (dare one say it) the nature of art (Marcuse 1978).

I do not quote extensively from the narratives of whistleblowers. If I were to do so to make my account more literary or even more satisfy-ing, it would mislead. Transformed into text, whistleblowers' narra-tives read more coherently than they sound.[1] This is, I believe, another reason that most books on whistleblowers mislead: the narrative ex-perience, filled with pauses, gaps, tears, and even moans, is inevitably smoothed out as it is retold by the author, even if the author puts quotes around his or her words, showing that they come from the whistleblower. They don't. Transformed into text, the whistleblower's words now belong to the author.

The transformation is unavoidable, and the only way to minimize it is to quote no more than is necessary to put the reader in the scene. Sometimes this is quite a lot, but the reader must remember the theo-retical point, which is not to allow the reader to enter vicariously into the world of the whistleblower (however satisfying that may be) but to know something of the forces that lead the whistleblower to lose the narrative thread. I have found narrative theory, which focuses on the form of the narrative, rather than content of the narrative, especially helpful.

Even so, there is one question about narrative content that can no longer be ignored. Were the whistleblowers telling the truth? I cross-checked the basic facts for most of the whistleblower stories in this and the last chapter. Some whistleblowers were subjects of newspaper or magazine articles. Others allowed me to talk with their lawyers, while still others presented me with trial transcripts, hearing transcripts, and the like. Whistleblowers generate a long paper trail. I did not investigate their cases, and I did not want to, but I generally checked to see that I was not being misled about the fundamentals of a case. I rarely was.

This, though, was the easy part. What about the more subtle questions, such as the whistleblower's claim that he did it for one reason and not another? How does one cross-check a motive? All one can do is judge whether a particular tale told by a whistleblower seeks to explain too much and experience too little. This is, I believe, the case with Ted's story.

A bunch of whistleblowers were sitting around wondering whether the experience had made them better persons. Most weren't sure. They'd learned much, but they'd become embittered, more difficult to live with, obsessed with their cases. Unable to contain himself any longer, Ted Greenbrook broke in. "I'm a new man. Every day I learn something good about myself."

> "But you said earlier that you lost your trust in authority," a whistleblower replied.
>
> "Yes, but now I believe in myself. Even though I lost my trust in authority, it restored my trust in myself. I believe in myself now. I don't need to believe in anybody else."

Ted protests too much. For that reason I distrust his account. This is not to say it is not true. His is a true account of his need to transform his suffering and loss into an experience of personal growth and enrichment. But I do not trust his ability to act as honest narrator of himself in the same way I do for some other whistleblowers. Mine is, one might respond, essentially a literary standard. That would be just the right response. Ted lacks the rich complexity of a convincing character, able to look at himself with gimlet eye. About stories, literary standards are the right ones. If, that is, we do not confuse literary standards with literary elegance, the narrative unity of the account that so often misleads.[2]

39

CHOICELESS CHOICE

"I did it because I had to ... because I had no other choice ... because I couldn't live with myself if I hadn't done anything ... because it was speak up or stroke out.... What else could I do? I have to look at myself in the mirror every morning?" This is what most whistleblowers say. I have strung the comments of several together to form a single quote.

Almost every whistleblower says this, and the question is how to regard this almost universal explanation, one that is generally offered gratis – that is, not in response to a question about "why'd you do it?" There is something formulaic about the explanation, but that does not mean empty. The trick will be to find out what the explanation is a formula for. The answer is that choiceless choice is a formula for relief from the almost unbearable regret of having let oneself be sent on a suicide mission.

Consider the parts of the self as actors in a narrative.[3] "Actants," they are called. The mark of the actant is that one person may play several roles; one person may play more than one actant. Actants are a class of actors with an identical relationship to the goal of action. Provide the actants with a plot, and we have a story. Let us call it the plot of plots – the structure of all narrative according to Algirdas Greimas (1983):

> A given order is *disturbed*.
>
> The *sender* establishes a *contract* with the *subject* to bring about a new order of things, or reinstate the old. The sender is an imparter of values, sending the subject on a quest.
>
> The subject becomes *competent* by virtue of values and attributes imparted by the sender: these may include the desire to restore order, the obligation to restore order, and the ability to restore order.
>
> The subject goes on a *quest* whose goal is to obtain the object for the benefit of the *receiver*.
>
> As the result of three basic tests, the subject fulfills his part of the contract and is rewarded, or fails to fulfill his contract and is punished.

The stereotypical love story exemplifies the plot of plots. He is both the subject and the receiver. She is both the object and the sender. Four actors (subject, receiver, object, sender) are incorporated into two actants. The merging of the sender with the object and the receiver with the subject occurs frequently, as in the love story: the subject's desire for the object is what sends him on his quest. It is for this reason that the sender is often called the power. But when the character of the subject is the main issue, the sender (power) merges with the subject. This is the case with every whistleblower narrative.

The sender is the whistleblower's character and values; the subject is the whistleblower in the role of organization man or woman. Choiceless choice is what happens when the sender speaks to the subject in a voice the subject cannot resist. In fact, it is useful to think about the sender as the power of the beloved. We understand what it is to be bewitched by love. How much more compelling it is to be bewitched by one's own values and beliefs. How much more difficult it is to escape that Siren's call. Deliver me from this kind of love the Greek prayed, and for good reason. More than one whistleblower wishes he had the foresight to tie himself to the mast, though Jim Bower did not put it quite that way. "If I knew then what I know now, I'd have told my wife to shoot me before letting me call [my congressman's] office."

Not many of us know what it is like to be overwhelmed by our own beliefs. Not, perhaps, because we have not been, but because this type of freedom comes frighteningly close to compulsion, so we blink and call it choice. Some whistleblowers experience the sender as a virtual dictator, destroying their lives and then walking away, leaving the subject to pick up the pieces. If it is the contract between sender and subject that explains choiceless choice, it is a contract between unequals. But then love was always like that, says Plato, desire a virtual slave to its object (Symposium, 203b–e). "I loved my job," said one whistleblower, "but it was nothing compared to how much I loved the job I gave myself, protector of the public. Now I don't have either. It reminds me of when my parents died, one right after the other."

In "What Is Freedom?" Hannah Arendt (1956, 151) argues that freedom is acting from a principle. "Action, to be free, must be free from motive on the one side, from its intended goal as a predictable effect on the other." Our motives are more likely to control us than vice versa. And the results of our acts depend on events far from our control. Only when we give ourselves over to our principles are we free. By the term "principles" Arendt means an idea or value that inspires us from "without," from the outside in. We do not make our principles. Our principles make us. This sense of the term "principle" is identical to what I am calling the sender.

Jim Bower continued, "Once I blew the whistle, I was free. I could breathe for the first time in years." Better than Arendt, the whistleblower knows that this freedom does not last. Or if it does, it is because he or she has had to rethink the meaning of freedom. "I was free to say what I thought was right, and now I am not free to work in my career. When was I more free, then or now?" Bower does not know.

Most of us think that freedom is about having and making choices. Arendt comes closer to the truth, writing about freedom as though it were a surrender to principle. But even this is an idealization as far as the whistleblower is concerned. The whistleblower understands that the freedom he has experienced comes closer to a compulsion, one that can seize a person and not let go until it has destroyed just about everything else the whistleblower cared about: career, home, family.

Bower concluded: "I'm glad I didn't have a choice. I don't think I could live with myself if I thought I chose all this." One might argue that this statement "proves" Bower had a choice, that his experience of compulsion is a way of avoiding responsibility for the consequences of his acts. It could be; these things are impossible to know for sure. One might, however, as easily conclude that the reader who cannot believe Bower was compelled may be defending him or her self against the possibility of such a threatening experience – that one could lose everything one cares about after being seized by an overpowering principle, almost as though it were a god.

Was Jim Bower too loyal to a principle, a principle that was insufficiently loyal to him – that is, insufficiently complex to take all of his interests as a person into account? I do not know. I do know that senders are often like that. How can one live with someone who is so terribly loyal to his principles that they can make mincemeat of everything else he or she cares about? How, in other words, can one live with the kind of person who is the sender to oneself – that is the subtext of most whistleblower narratives.

If the sender is supposed to make the subject competent, then it is a strange competence indeed, one that renders the whistleblower unable to perform that most basic American act – making a living from one's chosen career. But perhaps there are other things about which it is more important to be competent. And if the subject is rewarded for fulfilling his part of the contract, as he does, then we shall have to ask, What sort of reward is it to lose career, home, and family? One would hope that the whistleblower is rewarded with a deeper satisfaction, but it is precisely this that proves so elusive.

Choiceless choice is as close as many whistleblowers get to evaluating their own narratives.[4] Evaluation is not about stating the moral of the story. Evaluation is about telling the story in such a way that the listener comes to believe that it has a point, that it starts somewhere, stops somewhere else, and that one has learned something along the way. Evaluation, says William Labov (1972, 366), is "the means used by the narrator to indicate the point of the narrative, its raison d'être: why it was told and what the narrator was getting at. . . . When his narrative is over, it should be unthinkable for a bystander to say, 'So what?' "

The most effective evaluations are not tacked on but embedded in the story itself. Often this is done by the use of comparators (Labov 1972, 380–87; Pratt 1977, 49). Comparators move away from the story line for a moment to consider unrealized possibilities, comparing them with events that did occur, as in "If I hadn't blown the whistle, who knows where I would be today. The boss's office, maybe, or the grave." Comparators give the listener the feeling that humans with choices are involved, that life is a drama, not just a sequence of events. Comparators are the mark of a more fluid inner discourse.

Choiceless choice is a comparator in disguise. It seems to be saying, "I had no choice, so comparing alternatives is pointless." In fact, choiceless choice is a strong but undiscursive comparator, letting us know the strength of the sender, compared to which the whistleblower was powerless, as though he were sent to fight an angel or a devil. Choiceless choice makes whistleblowing an agony, a struggle between sender and receiver. That may sound a little abstract. Senders and receivers aren't yet flesh-and-blood characters. But sender and receiver are actors, and the struggle between them makes a world. This is more meaningful than the next theme, trapped in chronological time, in which actors become patients, to use Claude Bremond's term (Prince 1987, 69).

NARRATIVES STUCK IN STATIC TIME

For the first several months I attended the whistleblower support group, I thought that most of the men and women there had recently blown the whistle or had been recently fired. Their recall appears total, their emotional reaction as real as though it had happened today. In fact, many were talking about events that happened five to ten years ago and often longer than that. It is not as if nothing happens in the intervening years, but what happens is organized strictly by chronology. First this happened, then that, then that.

My boss did this, the company did that, then they committed this outrage, then they did that, and that, and that. Joseph Chaine put it this way: "First they moved my office to what used to be a broom closet, then they took away my computer, and finally they had me wrapping packages. I came in one day and my desk was piled high with other people's reports and a note that I was to wrap them and mail them. They even gave me the wrapping paper and a felt tip pen. And after I did that. . . ." This message came from a nuclear physicist at the Department of Energy who blew the whistle on his agency's misuse of computer simulations. Such accounts feel bereft of meaning, one act becoming equivalent to another in an endless chain of abasement.

Sometimes the chronology has the quality of a boxing match. "They called me downtown and tried to threaten me, I went to the MSPB [Merit System Protection Board], they put me on a twenty-one-day suspension, I hired a lawyer, they fired me, I slapped them with a lawsuit."

Box Boxer is an actor, not a patient, but his story does not feel any more meaningful. It feels like an endless cycle, a narrative turned in on itself, a never-ending story.

What makes meaning? In trying to make sense of why chronological accounts feel bereft of meaning, we may better answer this question: What makes some narratives more meaningful than others? In a cheap detective story, meaning inheres in the plot. Who done it? In more complex stories, real human stories, meaning seems to inhere in character development. Or rather, plot and character development are one. The *Bildungsroman* represents their union, but the conjunction of plot and character development is not restricted to that genre. What marks a static narrative, stuck in chronological time, is the way in which it subtly substitutes sequence for plot, including the plot that is character development. The result is a narrative stuck in static time.

Chronology is not an alternative to meaning. The king died, and then the queen died, to use E. M. Forster's (1927) example, is a meaningful story. Chronology is the imposition of a powerful, primordial meaning structure on chaos and fragmentation. Chronology is both the alternative to fragmentation and another form of it, sequential fragmentation, the fragments ordered into line, like a cold and ragged queue of strangers who don't even share the time of day.

Against chronology one wants to oppose plot. The king died, and then the queen died of grief, to use Forster's example again, is the simplest plot, one event causing another. The trouble is that many whistleblowers swing from chronology to plot with a vengeance, from mere sequence to plots in which everything is meaningfully connected to everything else, the theme I call paranoia. What is needed is another form of metonymy, another way of connecting the pieces.

Metonymy is a figure of speech whereby a term designating one notion, A, is used for another term designating another notion, B, that is related to A as cause and effect, container and contained, or part and whole. Metonymy is a principle of contiguity and connection that includes more than sequence and cause, but generally not mere metaphor. Some narratologists argue that narrative is predominantly metonymic, sequences connected not only by contiguity but by motifs (Prince 1987, 52).

What whistleblowers need is a way of connecting the pieces that is more meaningful than chronology but not as totally meaningful as paranoia, in which everything is causally connected to everything else. Motifs would be a good example of a looser connection, along the lines of Jim Joiner's comment: "First my boss fired me for getting involved, then my girlfriend gave me the pink slip for not paying enough attention to her." Joiner has made a connection, but it is not causal (he does not imagine that his boss threatened his girlfriend so she should leave him, as in a paranoid narrative), nor is it merely chronological: the motif of getting fired has become symbolically enlarged to encompass several different types of exile. The last theme considered, "living in the position of the dead," represents a similarly enlarged motif.

Before continuing, we must address an objection – that we are all stuck in static time. Particularly about the major events of our lives, such as weddings, births, and funerals, we replay all the old tapes again and again. We want to; sometimes we want to be stuck in time in a world that moves too fast. It is true enough, and shortly I will consider that whistleblowers may have found their chronological recitations soothing.

One could argue that it is strictly a matter of degree. Whistleblowers are more stuck in static time than the rest of us. The real difference, however, is more subtle. Whistleblowers use chronology as a substitute for plot and as an alternative to meaningful motifs. Whistleblowers cling to chronology not to slow the world down but to keep it from falling apart. They have experienced a disaster, and the disaster threatens to make the world meaningless. Chronology is meaning, albeit a particularly one-dimensional one. It is the meaning that remains when the narrator is not fully present in his own story.

Only once did I hear a whistleblower become aware of the meaningless of the chronological structure of her narrative. It came as a revelation to her. "You know," she said, "I've been talking about what happened to me for over an hour now, and I just realized. It doesn't mean anything, it doesn't mean a damn thing. It's just a list, like the grocery list I made last night. What matters is what it did to me inside, and I haven't begun to figure that part out yet."

In The Writing of the Disaster, Maurice Blanchot (1995, 7) is concerned with the way in which the disaster de-scribes, making writing (and telling) about it almost impossible. By disaster, Blanchot means those experiences that disrupt our experience of going on being with the world so that we cannot put ourselves and the world back together again. The Holocaust is paradigmatic, but we live in a world of disaster, whose mark is that we cannot weave a meaningful story around it. We cannot weave a story because we have lost the place from which to speak. That place is the present.

The narrative voice may speak from past and future, inside the story and outside. The power of narrative stems from the narrator's ability to be there and then, as well as here and now. But the implied author (not the narrator but the one whose existence is implied from the design of the story) must be present, and feel present, for the listener to share the story. This is especially true for spoken narrative, in which speaker and listener are in each other's presence, but it is as true of a two-thousand-year-old text.

If, that is, we understand presence in its dual sense of contemporaneous, as well as intellectually or emotionally available, accessible, knowable. Plato may not be contemporaneous, but he is present as implied author in those dialogues (actually narratives) in which Socrates is the narrator. We puzzle about the relationship between Plato and Socrates, but that is precisely the point. Both are present to us.

The disaster de-scribes because it destroys not chronology but the meaningful experience of time. Chronology substitutes for the experience of going on being, as the psychoanalyst D. W. Winnicott (1958, 304), one of the authors cited by Blanchot, puts it. Chronology is the defense against time that has lost its meaning, probably because life has lost its meaning. Mere chronology takes the place of an experience of time as flow that carries us with it, which is why strictly chronological narratives feel so wooden. Time loses its meaning because the present no longer holds, in the sense of being a place that it is possible to be, because the I is no longer present to be there.

The "presentiment of something which is nothing" is how Søren Kierkegaard (1957, 38) defines dread. We may think about dread as something terrible, but that is not how dread is experienced. Dread is experienced as no-thing, an experience that is void because we are unable to put it in a story. As Blanchot (1995, 15, 29) puts it, "When the subject becomes absence, then the absence of a subject . . . subverts the whole sequence of existence, causes time to take leave of its order. . . . Time has radically changed its meaning and its flow. Time without present, I without I."

Narrative goes all over the place in time and space, speaking in dozens of voices, but it still needs the present presence of an I to tell it.

Narratives that lack presence feel vicarious, somehow unreal, as if the teller were not fully there. *The Stranger*, by Albert Camus, achieves its literary power from the exploitation of this effect, Meursault strangely absent from his own story (Pratt 1972, 189–90). Many whistleblower narratives have this same quality. The difference is that

47

the whistleblower is not a character in a novel, so it becomes useful to ask what happened to the whistleblower so that his story feels unreal.

What has happened is that the whistleblower has become Scherherazade, desperately keeping the story going lest disaster strike: the disaster of having nothing more to say because the story is finally over. "And then they didn't do anything else because it was over." To say this is to be abandoned by one's persecutors to a faithless world, which is why so few whistleblowers can say it. Jim Beam put it this way: "Any time I'd say something bad about them to the newspapers, they [the company that fired him] used to sic their lawyers on me. Now they don't even respond when I threaten to sue them. I'm starting to think I don't exist."

"The turbulence of stagnant motion" is how another whistleblower described his years of exile. It is also a good description of narratives stuck in static time, filled with meaningless motion, an endless sequence of events, because the storyteller cannot bear to bring the story to an end and so finally know its meaning.

Stories are defined by their end. Everything that happens before is reinterpreted in light of how it all turns out in the end. Without an ending, there can be no plot and hence no satisfactory meaning – which is precisely why whistleblowers cannot bear to end their stories. One could argue that it is because the whistleblower *doesn't* know the meaning of his story that he cannot bring to a stop the endless sequence of events. On the contrary, I argue that it is precisely because he *does* know that he cannot find the end. Then he would have to learn the meaning of what he already knows. That, evidently, is almost unbearable.[5]

"Our ability to gain access to these narratives depends on what we are prepared to forsake to listen to them," says Langer (1991, 195). He is writing about listening to the narratives of Holocaust survivors, but it applies to whistleblowers too. This is not because whistleblowers have suffered similarly. The suffering of survivors exceeds that of whistleblowers by orders of magnitude. Indeed, this is precisely the point.

Not as wounded as the survivor, the whistleblower is more likely to just keep talking so that he himself will not have to give up the truths of common narrative, the stock stories we all draw on to make at least superficial sense of our lives. The "little man who stood up against the big corporation and won" is a common narrative. Common narratives are not lies. They are more like clichés, worn and out-of-context truths, insufficiently complex to account for experience.

KNOWLEDGE AS DISASTER

To know what he has already learned, the whistleblower would have to give up what every right-thinking American believes in. To forsake this is particularly difficult for the largest group of whistleblowers I listened to: conservative middle-aged men. "Hell, I wasn't against the system," said Bob Warren. "I was the system. I just didn't realize there were two systems."

What must the whistleblower forsake in order to hear his own story?

– That the individual matters.

– That law and justice can be relied on.

– That the purpose of law is to remove the caprice of powerful individuals.

– That ours is a government of laws, not men.

– That the individual will not be sacrificed for the sake of the group.

– That loyalty isn't equivalent to the herd instinct.

– That one's friends will remain loyal even if one's colleagues do not.

– That the organization is not fundamentally immoral.

– That it makes sense to stand up and do the right thing. (Take this literally: that it "makes sense" means that it is a comprehensible activity.)

– That someone, somewhere, who is in charge knows, cares, and will do the right thing.

– That the truth matters, and someone will want to know it.

– That if one is right and persistent, things will turn out all right in the end.

– That even if they do not, other people will know and understand.

– That the family is a haven in a heartless world. Spouses and children will not abandon you in your hour of need.

– That the individual can know the truth about all this, not become merely cynical, cynical unto death.

Not only is it hard to come to terms with these truths, but when one finally does, it seems one is left with nothing. "My case is not griev-

49

able," said Bob Warren. He meant that it was not subject to further grievance procedures, but one might think about it another way. Bob could not feel the appropriate grief because to do so he would have to learn too much about what he already knew.

Or consider the case of Joseph Rose, who exposed the Associated Milk Producers' illegal contributions to Nixon's reelection campaign. "I believe I can make a contribution to the young people in this country by continuing to respond with a strong warning that all of the public utterances of corporations, and indeed, our own government concerning 'courage, integrity, loyalty, honesty, and duty' are nothing but the sheerest hogwash" (Glazer and Glazer 1989, 223). How in the world could one want to teach this to schoolchildren and not be possessed by cynicism? Rose would teach a lesson as bitter as his heart.

"Knowledge as disaster" is how Blanchot puts it. Not knowledge of the disaster, but knowledge as disaster, because it cannot be contained within existing frames and forms of experience, including common narrative. The result is that Bob Warren is stuck in chronological time, an oxymoron that isn't once one considers that chronological time may be experienced as a respite from the end of time, or at least the end of the story, when one must finally know its meaning.

"I just can't live with myself knowing what I know," said Amy Brown with a long sigh. "I just have to do something about it." She finally did, but I can't get beyond the first part of her statement, the one before the sigh-as-caesura. Amy Brown is a psychologist who went to the FBI over Medicaid fraud committed by her previous employer. (Medicaid fraud is the single biggest source of whistleblowers' complaints.) Her boss went to jail, but she couldn't get a job in the state where she worked. "They were all afraid I might commit the truth," she said. Eventually she moved across the country. "My new colleagues, the ones who didn't know my story, kept asking me if I had been violated in some way. They meant rape or assault. There must be something about the way I carried myself, like I was scared of being intruded upon or something."

Amy Brown was violated by knowledge. The violation is the knowledge, knowledge as violation. Ordinarily we think of knowledge as something gained. But what if the gain implies losses we can hardly bear? The unwanted knowledge of the way the world really works invaded Amy Brown, possessed her, and the only way for her to be free would be to give up the truths of common narrative. She is headed in that direction, but it will take a while.

Being vindicated, as Amy Brown was, is not enough, and now we are in a position to see why. What is the satisfaction in being right if as a consequence one has to give up everything one believed in?

Another whistleblower, a nurse who reported an extreme case of Medicare fraud at her old job, had to quit her new job when she discovered that the home health care company she went to work for was bending the rules regarding patients' eligibility for Medicare. I told her I thought she quit because she couldn't stand being a whistleblower again. No, she said. "That's not it. I could do that. What I can't stand is thinking that everybody cheats."

Or consider the case of Mike Quint, an engineer who exposed defects and cover-ups in the construction of tunnels to be used by Los Angeles Metro Rail. Since Los Angeles is the site of frequent earthquakes, shortcuts in building the tunnels endangered hundreds of lives. Though Quint was eventually fired from the construction management company that oversaw the building of the tunnels, he persisted in his letter-writing campaign. As a result, the construction management company was removed from the project, the tunnel contractor performed remedial work taking eight months, and several employees of the Los Angeles Metro Rail went to jail.

Quint takes little satisfaction in his victory. Not only does he say he wouldn't do it again, but he has turned into something of a zombie on his new job. Whistleblowing "has reduced my trust and faith in people and in our justice system.... I [now] expect fewer benefits from work, and perform my duties as directed, with fewer questions of decisions or procedures" (Miethe 1999, 161–62).

Why does Quint despair? He was right, the *Los Angeles Times* made sure everyone knew it, and he has a job in his field again. It must be his perverse choice to see the glass as half empty when he could just as well see it as half full. Or so the distant observer might think.

What if Quint has lost the glass? What if he has lost the container that held everything he cared about and valued, what he calls his trust and faith in people. These are simple words, but what if they really mean something? For some, the earth moves when they discover that people in authority routinely lie and that those who work for them routinely cover up. Once one knows this, or rather once one feels this knowledge in one's bones, one lives in a new world. Some people remain aliens in the new world forever. Maybe they like it that way. Maybe they don't have a choice.

What is the meaning of life? To this little question Freud answered, love and work, an answer that by now is almost a cliché (Erikson 1963). What happens when the world becomes unlovable and our work impossible? One might argue that the world can never become unlovable. We just need to try harder. But this does not seem to be Freud's position. If love is not just a psychic discharge but a way of being in the world, then that way of being "demands that the world present itself to us as worthy of our love" (Lear 1990, 153). If love is not just a feeling but the force that makes the world go around, as Freud speculated in his later works (and as Plato imagined in *The Symposium*), then loving the world and being able to love the world because the world is lovable are two sides of the same coin. We make the world meaningful with our love, and the world makes our lives meaningful by being lovable. When one partner fails, both do. The meaning of life depends on our ability to remain in a love affair with the world. Like any long-term love affair, this means that the world must love us back, even if this only means remaining worthy of our love.

It will not do to encourage the whistleblower to try harder. He or she must find alternative sources of meaning – other aspects of the world that remain worthy of love. Paranoia is one way in which this search for love gets derailed. In paranoia, everything becomes meaningful, which is about as bad as a world in which nothing is meaningful. Paranoia and despair are two sides of the same coin.

PARANOID THEMES

Like the rest of us, whistleblowers live between paranoia and despair: between a world in which everything is meaningfully connected to oneself and a world in which nothing is. Sometimes individual whistleblowers lose the balance; most do not.[6] Especially fascinating is the way the whistleblower support group indulged its paranoia, but only to a point. Members could imagine government conspiracies in general, but particular ones made them nervous.

Mary Nummer, an infrequent visitor to the group, told a story that became increasingly paranoid. She lost her job as a government auditor because she went to her boss's boss over some improperly documented payment vouchers. Thus began a chain that went from losing her house and husband, being stalked, sideswiped and rear-ended in a series of collisions with black sedans, and finally having everything stolen from her locked apartment, which was located in a poor section of town.

Mary never explicitly said the events were connected with her blowing the whistle, but that was the implication, informed by her numerology: five years after she was fired she crashed a five-thousand-dollar car, seven years after she was fired she lived on the seventh floor of an apartment with seven locks that was broken into, and so forth.

Usually eager for a paranoid story (it makes life interesting, the work of being a whistleblower important), the group members began to squirm, finding an excuse to go out and get a drink or whatever. Finally Janet Docent spoke up. "I understand. When you're a whistleblower you get fired and suffer a loss of income. This means you move down the social ladder and become victim to all the criminals who prey on the lower classes."

In three sentences Janet had normalized the experience, and another whistleblower took the stage, one whose paranoia was more within bounds – that is, no greater than that of most who write social theory or read it. He told a story of being unable to find work as a nuclear engineer because the industry maintains an informal blacklist.

If narrative is built on the exploitation of the *post hoc ergo propter hoc* fallacy, as Roland Barthes (1975) argues, then paranoid narratives are the most narrative of narratives. Nothing just follows, everything is causally connected, and the whistleblower is the prime mover. Like the more well-known Prime Mover, the whistleblower is strangely absent from the chain of events he or she has set in motion. Nominally an internal narrator, the whistleblower talks more like an external narrator, telling us from a position of vast remove about a world that considers him terribly important.

One gains new respect for paranoia from listening to whistleblowers' narratives. This is not because "even paranoids have real enemies," as the cliché goes. It is true, but it is not the point. Chronology finds meaning only in sequence because the flow of experience has been lost. Paranoia finds meaning everywhere. Paranoia is a surfeit of meaning, the world overflowing with meaning. Paranoia is the will to meaning. Or rather, paranoia is a last desperate attempt to flood the world with meaning. Paranoia is a defense against loss of meaning, the same loss of meaning that is the source of dread.

One more element of the paranoid narrative deserves discussion, but it is hard to know how to describe it, except to say that the paranoid whistleblower is absolutely right. Not about the details, like the manager who may have smashed the windows of the whistleblower's car. About the details it is hard to know. The paranoid whistleblower is absolutely right that his organization is not just out to fire him but to obliterate him or her. The whistleblower's paranoia is an accurate emotional reading of an emotional reality: the one who has become the scapegoat cannot just be dismissed but must be destroyed, so that others will know.

Marjorie Gooden put it this way: "After mom got from fired from the Department of Agriculture for being a whistleblower, I think she went a little crazy. Mom thought the car that ran her off the road was from her agency. But, you know, after a while I realized that they did want to kill her. Not really, but they wanted to make it as if she had never existed, that everything she said had never happened. That's a type of murder too." It is the worst kind according to Orwell in *Nineteen Eighty-Four*: to have the record of one's life shoved down the memory hole, as though one had never existed.

It is this aspect of paranoia that is the most difficult of all for an outsider to come to terms with because it represents a truth that is hard to know: that if the organization feels sufficiently threatened by the individual, it will remove him, not just beyond the margins of the organization but all the way to the margins of society. The average whistleblower of my experience is a fifty-five-year-old nuclear engineer working behind the counter at Radio Shack. Divorced and in debt to his lawyers, he lives in a two-room rented apartment. He has no retirement plan and few prospects for advancement.

Because the power to marginalize is so frightening, it is easier to attribute paranoia to the whistleblower, rather than to see the whistleblower as a prophet: not just in what he or she has to say about waste, fraud, and abuse but what he or she has learned in crossing the frontier between loyalty and morality. It is not a reality that is easily expressed in words. It is the paranoid form of the narrative that comes closest to this truth.

My reaction to a story told by Molly Higgins may help explain this. A self-described military wife, Molly is married to Tom, a pilot who lost his career for protesting the failure of the military to live up to the law regarding the education of disabled children of military personnel.[7]

After Tom wrote to his congressman about his son's poor education, the air force sent him for psychiatric observation. This is standard procedure, the quickest, easiest way to separate someone from the military (until just recently it was the quickest and easiest way to separate any federal worker). In short order, Tom was decertified from flying and transferred to a remote base where he was given a desk job keeping track of spare parts. A series of bad efficiency reports followed. After being sent for yet another psychiatric examination, Tom was confined for several days in a military hospital. He was separated from the military when he was less than a year from retirement. The whole process took about three years from the day Tom wrote his congressman.

One might argue that Tom Higgins *was* unstable, and certainly somewhere along the way he may have become so. But no one found him unstable until he wrote his congressman, after trying for several years to get his child placed in special education. (His letter is temperate.) It was then that Tom entered the machine whose product is the elimination of the whistleblower in ways entirely compatible with the law.

Molly Higgins watched all this, and in some ways she understands what has happened to her husband better than he does. She has become her broken husband's less broken voice. Tom is still somewhere in the machine. Molly says:

55

> We were a good military family. We thought it was a misunderstand-
> ing.... When I was a girl I grew up near an Air Force base, and I loved
> to see the big birds come in. When I met my husband and he told me he
> owned one, it was love at first sight. I was the most patriotic girl who
> ever was, born in a small town, white. I didn't know what happens to
> you if you end up on the other side.

What happens?

> They kill you, they isolate you in the desert. We weren't traitors. We
> were trying to get the best education for our kid. I lost it there for a
> while. I lost something to be proud of. I lost faith in God. We were too
> far North. [Her husband's last posting had been to a base near the arc-
> tic circle.] You know, we wanted it exposed, what the military was doing
> to the children. But we were the ones who were exposed, and now it will
> never be the same. Now I don't believe in anything.

Why not believe in something else?

> I do, I believe in what I learned. You have to go one step at a time, one
> day at a time, take back what's yours. I've lost my virginity. I can't say
> bad is good anymore.

There was nothing especially paranoid about Molly's story. More
paranoid was my reaction. It just can't be true, I kept saying to myself. Tom must have been basically unstable for all this to happen.
The military wouldn't do this, it wouldn't have forcibly hospitalized
him for three days just to give him a negative psychiatric evaluation
so as to decertify him from flying. There must be something else
going on here.

What if there is not? Or what if there is, but it does not matter, because there would not have been anything else had Tom not written his
congressman? What if this is the way it works, and the interviewer can
hardly bear to know it. So the interviewer too invokes a strategy of
common narrative, along the following lines: "OK, his kid wasn't getting the education he was entitled to, but Tom shouldn't have written
his congressman. Even so, the military wouldn't have done all that to
him unless there really was something else wrong with him. The system isn't that relentless." What if it is?

"LIVING IN THE POSITION OF THE DEAD"

The cleverness with which the whistleblower support group acted to normalize an extreme case of paranoia led me to consider a disturbing possibility. Maybe the whistleblowers knew more about what they were doing than I did. Maybe there was an unspoken permanent agenda among the whistleblowers to which I was not privy. With the term "unspoken permanent agenda," Labov (1972, 370) refers to the way in which the context and point of the story are set by the expectations of the listeners, not just the narrator. Among the young men Labov studied, a fight narrative was always on the agenda. It was "felt to be tellable," simply because it was about a fight. One did not have to explain the point; it already had one.

Sometimes it seemed to me that the point of the whistleblower support group was to experience pleasure in hearing the same old stories, whether told by old members or new, over and over again. I became impatient, wanting to ask, "So, what's the point? What's next? What did you learn? How are you going to use what you learned on the rest of your life's journey?" But this was my agenda, an instrumental one, albeit in the service of life. Sometimes it seemed to me that the whistleblowers had another agenda – taking pleasure in the same old stories, in which the soothing meaninglessness of chronology was relieved by the overstimulating meaning of paranoia. There was, in other words, a contract between the whistleblowers to which I had not signed on. What I took as narrative forms that risked imprisoning the whistleblowers, they experienced as forms that held and comforted them. Or so I sometimes suspected.

Since this is my story as much as theirs, I will continue with my argument, recognizing the possibility that whistleblowers might see it differently because they are operating from a different agenda. One reason I believe that I am right (which does not make the whistleblowers wrong) is because I occasionally came across a whistleblower whose narrative didn't sound stuck or imprisoned. The difference was striking. Most whistleblowers' narratives seemed stuck in time or imprisoned in a closed universe in which everything refers to everything else, with nothing left over for the world. A few whistleblowers sounded free, but hardly in the conventional sense.

One expression of this freedom was the freedom of one "who lives as already dead," as the Japanese put it (Benedict 1946, 248–50). Though I never heard an American whistleblower use this term, I heard the idea several times. To live as if one is already dead is what is said about a Japanese who has suffered a terrible experience of shame, humiliation, and loss and lived through it. The term may also be used as an admonition. When a Japanese student is about to take an exam, his friend may say, "Be as one already dead." The term implies a supreme release from conflict: between the desire to be free and the desire to fit in and serve. To live as if one were already dead is to live free of self-watchfulness, self-surveillance, and constant concern with what other people think, a concern of us all and a special concern to some Japanese.

"One day I realized I didn't care what people thought any more. I make barely enough to live on, but I can tell the truth about anything." Joe Wahlreich said this, a lawyer who now cleans the building whose basement he lives in order to make ends meet. This was as close as I heard a whistleblower come to living in the position of the dead. His freedom was, I believe, Wahlreich's reward for having fulfilled his contract with the sender. Finally he was free of its terrible power because its demands could no longer destroy his life. His sender had done its best (or worst), and Joe was still standing.

Recall the problem of metonymy: how to link narrative episodes in ways that are neither strictly chronological nor causal. Living in the position of the dead has more the quality of container and contained, another metonymic relationship. First one is enveloped by death, then one becomes the death by which one was enveloped and so goes on to live in a new way.

Wu-wei is a Taoist term meaning nonaction but better rendered as action that is in accord with nature. Living in the position of the dead is wu-wei. Perhaps it is not really a reversal of container and contained. Perhaps it is more akin to mimesis, becoming the disaster so as not to be destroyed by it. I believe this is what Blanchot (1995, 41) means when he says, "The danger [is] that the disaster acquire meaning instead of body." To become disaster's body is to live in the position of the dead.

To know the truth behind the veil, the truth that not only is concealed by common narrative but antithetical to it, is already to be in the position of the dead. To know it is already to be socially dead – that is, unable fully to be present with those who do not know it. For it is to know that most of the things people value about society are already dead, lost illusions.

"You know what's different now?" Joe Wahlreich asked. "It's a funny thing, a little thing really, but it feels like a big one. I can't make small talk anymore. When I hear someone saying the little things people say every day, I get impatient. I want to say to them, 'Look, open your eyes. People around you are living in hell, and you don't even notice.' I was in hell and no one noticed. I didn't either, not for years. You can't get out of hell until you know you're there."

Where are you now?

"Purgatory, I guess. And you know what? That's as good as it's going to get for me. I know too much to ever get into heaven."

For Joe, getting into purgatory meant living in the position of the dead.

For another whistleblower, Martin Edwin Andersen, getting into purgatory has meant accepting that he had accomplished something very different from what he set out to do with his life.[8]

> I've always wanted to be somebody, but I guess I should have been more specific. . . . Integrity – what should be a minimum requisite for public service – has become instead your specific, and perhaps only real, memorable contribution to the workplace. Forget your years of professional preparation for greater challenges and greater recognition; forget the sacrifices you and your parents have made to get where you are, and forget your fondest dreams of advancement. The bottom line is that when you look around, your career is stalled, and you feel alone.

One is reminded of Polemarchus, a character in Plato's *Republic* (331d–334c), who learns from Socrates that justice isn't just one profession among many but a just man's only true calling. In this world that knowledge can feel cold as hell.

CONCLUSION

Is living in the position of the dead a coda or a resolution? If we see it as a coda, then we will emphasize the way it serves to bring the story back to the present, the purpose of the coda (Labov 1972, 365–66). If we see it as a resolution, then we will see it as the whistleblower's successful attempt to escape the prison of static time, albeit in a way that is most ironic. By living in the position of the dead, the whistleblower becomes subject to infinity – that is, endless time. This, though, may be taking the phrase too literally. Because living in the position of the dead is the way in which Joe Wahlreich has found new meaning in his life, it is probably most accurate to see it as a resolution, through which he returns to the world of meaningful experience, albeit in a way he had never imagined, as a passionate bystander.

Most whistleblowers' narratives lack a resolution. They just go on and on, not because the whistleblower lacks the narrative skills to bring his story to an end but because the resources of common narrative are insufficient. The stories that most of us tell are too superficial, too dedicated to not looking, to be of much help to the whistleblower who has seen what one is not supposed to know.

So many Americans hate their government and distrust big corporations that one would think whistleblowers would find more understanding for their stories. After all, some whistleblowers become heroes, at least to a large segment of the public. A movie, *The Insider*, depicts a cigarette company executive who became a whistleblower (though even the movie devoted most of its attention to the producer who put him on television). "The little man who stood up against the big corporation and won" is a type of folk hero. But that is just the problem. He is a type of folk hero, that is, a stereotype. Everyone wants to hear about the stereotype, but no one wants to know how vulnerable we are to power and how much it can take from us, including the meaning of our lives. It is this the whistleblower has to teach, but no one wants to learn.

We may tell our own stories, but we cannot tell them to ourselves. We can tell them only if others are prepared to hear them in something resembling the terms in which they are told. (In the language of narratology, one can tell one's story only if the narratee is on the same diegetic level, which means sharing the terms of the fiction.[9]) What happens when the terms we most value, the terms of the sender, are not recognized by the world? What happens when principles for which one has ruined one's life are regarded by others as mere words?

One whistleblower responded this way: "I have seen the truth and the truth has made me odd."[10] Most whistleblowers would have to put it more strongly: "I have seen the truth, and the truth has shaken my belief in who I am because it has shaken my belief in the world I live in."

The ignorant reaction of the world to the whistleblower becomes a part of the whistleblower. The whistleblower becomes less at home in the world because the world is not an understanding place to be. It is this homelessness that is the present absence in narratives structured strictly by time, or flooded with paranoid meaning, that last desperate alternative to no meaning at all.

The suffering the whistleblower experiences has the quality of what Michel Foucault (1979) calls discipline. "Nuts and sluts" is the term many whistleblowers use to describe this disciplinary process, referring to the way those who raise ethical issues are treated as disturbed or morally suspect. About this discipline one cannot tell a story. Or at least one cannot tell a human story about a protagonist engaged in a quest. Discipline works through the language of science and medicine, in which actors become patients. In other words, discipline operates at a different diegetic level, its subjects transformed into objects, the topic of chapter 6.

Joe Klein struggled for years to make sense of what happened to him. An accountant for a large corporation, he'd gone to his boss about his suspicion that they were overcharging the government on a contract they were working on.

First thing, they sent me to the doctor, then they put me on medical leave, and when I tried to go back to work they told me I was too sick. Before I knew it they gave me early retirement, made me take it. Don't get me wrong, I got great benefits, better than if I'd kept my mouth shut, but it's not what I wanted. I wanted to do the right thing, save the government some money. Now I'm the one with the money and no job.

Joe Klein doesn't know if he's a victim, a hero, or a co-conspirator. Nor do I.

The failure of common narrative is not just a cultural failure. It is also a political failure, the failure of our society to address the isolation and sacrifice of the moral individual in this evidently most individual-

61

istic of societies. Narrative analysis can help us see this, and richer narrative forms can help us make sense of this experience. But such forms are dependent on the forces of power and production, just as culture is dependent, even as it is no mere superstructure. New narrative forms are unlikely to be forthcoming, at least on a large scale, in the absence of social and political change.

Neither whistleblowers nor the rest of us live in a world of wall-to-wall narrative, to paraphrase Edward Said. The whistleblower's narrative is not arrested because all narratives are arrested. The whistleblower's narrative is arrested because the whistleblower has had experiences that cannot be framed and formed within the resources of common narrative. These last remarks may seem obvious. They are aimed at those few academics who occasionally write as if narratives lived a life of their own.

CHAPTER 4

Whistleblower Ethics: Narcissism Moralized

My heart's fellow will love in me what You [Lord] tell us is lovable, deplore in me what You tell us is deplorable. – Saint Augustine, *Confessions*

A s you read this chapter and the next, I'm going to ask you to put aside all your prejudices against narcissism. Not because they are not true but because they are not the whole truth. Narcissists are often vain, self-aggrandizing, and immoral. But not always. Narcissism is also a deep and powerful source of morality, leading some narcissists to sacrifice all their worldly goods for a noble idea. What could be more moral than that?

The narcissist wants to be whole, good, pure, and perfect. There are two ways to do this. Either one lowers one's standards of wholeness, goodness, purity, and perfection until they correspond to one's miserable self. Or one raises one's miserable self as high as one possibly can so that one comes a little closer to these ideal standards. I call this second strategy narcissism moralized. It is exemplified in the quotation from Saint Augustine that opens this chapter.

Most whistleblowers I have encountered are motivated by narcissism moralized. One of the whistleblowers with whom I shared the manuscript of this book is still insulted by the term. Narcissism is probably not the most attractive motivation around, but I do not believe our task is to judge motives as much as it is to understand them. In any case, narcissism moralized gets the ethical job done, leading many whistleblowers to risk all but their lives so as not to be made less whole, pure, and good by corruption in the organizations they work for.[1]

Have I abandoned my pledge not to try to explain why whistleblowers do it? No. Explication is not explanation. In turning to narcissism moralized as an account of why whistleblowers do it, I am explicating a theme that describes what many whistleblowers said to me. I have no interest in why whistleblowers are more narcissistic than most people, if this is even the case. Where their narcissism moralized comes from is not my concern. I do not think I could find out even if I wanted to. Certainly I am not interested in the social psychological correlates of narcissism moralized. What whistleblowers said to me about why they did it is readily summarized under the category of moralized narcissism, and that is what I am reporting.

I am going to ask the reader to do one more thing. Accept, for the sake of argument (I also believe it is true) that many whistleblowers have acted ethically in the objective sense. That is, whatever one thinks of the whistleblower's motives, any reasonable person would agree to the following:

– It is ethical to tell the truth under oath, even when one is told not to do so by one's boss. That the whistleblower reasonably assessed the objective situation is demonstrated by the fact that the boss eventually went to jail.

– It is ethical to go up the chain of command about a dangerous nuclear reactor when the Atomic Energy Commission (AEC) will not act. That the whistleblower reasonably assessed the objective situation is demonstrated by the fact that the AEC eventually did act on the whistleblower's concern.

– It is ethical to testify to Congress about systematic overcharging by military contractors. That the whistleblower reasonably assessed the objective situation is demonstrated by the fact that some contractors went to jail.

All this may seem obvious, but it serves an important point. If I am going to claim that it is possible to learn something new about ethics from studying whistleblowers, the reader must agree that at least some whistleblowers have acted ethically in the objective sense. Then if we discover that their reasons do not correspond to the usual ethical categories (such as Kant's, or Carol Gilligan's [1982], for example), we will be in a position to ask if this does and should change our understanding of what constitutes an ethical motive. I am, in other words, asking the reader to hold the objective aspect of ethics constant, so we can study the subjective aspect.

In writing about ethics in this way, one must be careful not to try to derive ought from is. Because whistleblowers act ethically while talking about ethics in a way that does not accord with the usual ways of talking about ethics does not make whistleblowers right. One might logically (though, I believe, foolishly) hold that whistleblowers have acted objectively ethically while holding that their motives are not ethical. Narcissism cannot be a valid ethical motive no matter what, so whistleblowers cannot be ethical no matter how moralized their narcissism. Such a position, while philosophically coherent, would make of ethics an a priori enterprise, in which we define what constitutes a genuine subjectively ethical motive and judge people accordingly. It would assume that we could not reconsider what constitutes an ethical motive in light of ethical behavior.

FIVE STORIES

Whistleblowers tell five types of stories about why they did it. They tell others, of course, but these seem to be the main ones. In each, the subject tries to explain the experience of choiceless choice to him or herself. How did I find myself in the strange position where this is all I could do? In one way or another, this is the question each whistleblower is addressing.

Not every whistleblower offered his or her story as an explicit attempt to explain his or her experience of choiceless choice. I am reporting on conversations among whistleblowers, and like all conversations they jump around a bit. Nevertheless, I believe this was almost always the implicit context. Not just "Why did I do it?" but "How did I get myself into a situation where this was all I could do?"

The narrative structure is always the same, a conversation of voices within the whistleblower, the voice that compelled explaining to the voice that acted why it had no choice. In all five stories, the whistleblower is both subject and object, the storyteller and the one the story is about. In all five stories the subject knows himself to be the sender. In all five, the storyteller is more than a little chagrined at the intransigence of his subject sender, himself or herself. Together these stories go some way to explaining the experience of choiceless choice, not just to me but to the whistleblowers themselves.

65

All five stories can readily be interpreted in terms of traditional moral categories, such as obligation, duty, and loyalty to principle over person. Such an interpretation would be far from false. These are relevant categories, but they are not the whole story. After narrating these five stories, I interpret them in terms that do not fit the usual ethical categories. While narcissism moralized is not a familiar ethical category, it should become one.

The stories here are not as constricted as the narratives analyzed in the previous chapter, even though some are told by the same whistleblowers. This has mostly to do with differences in the circumstances in which I heard the stories. The narratives of the last chapter were produced with very little questioning from me, while the responses in this chapter were more often answers to my questions. I engaged the whistleblowers about their choices, providing a space I invited them to fill. This approach seemed to focus the whistleblower's response.

This was not necessarily good, or even the best way to learn about whistleblower ethics, but it seemed necessary. Whistleblowers spontaneously talk about their cases; they do not spontaneously reflect on their ethics. Whistleblowers did, however, seem to enjoy talking about their ethics. They were talking about a part of their experience that was somehow easier to come to terms with: not what they had learned and who they had become but who they once were and what they valued. This too may have contributed to the smoother flow of these stories.

An Imagination for Consequences

"I am afflicted by my imagination for consequences" is how Tom Delaney put it. Tom blew the whistle on the Department of Energy's failure to clean up properly an abandoned research site.

"I just couldn't stop imagining what would happen if children climbed over the fence and played in the radioactive dust."

"What about your colleagues?" asked another whistleblower. "Were they too scared to protest?"

"I don't think so," the engineer replied. "They just didn't think about it. Site protection was not our responsibility. It really wasn't my job. My job was just to shut [the old reactor] down. I just couldn't stop thinking about it. My boss said to keep my mind on my job. He meant don't think about what you are doing. I did, and I lost my job."

Tom is currently working as a courier, delivering legal papers around town. He sounds ashamed, as though he has failed in some way. If he could have just kept his mind on his job, he would have done fine. He seems to feel he is a prisoner of his almost visceral connection to the long-term consequences of his acts.

Hannah Arendt (1978b, 3:257) writes about training your imagination to go visiting. It is, she suspects, the ground of all ethics, the ability to take others into account. Only in Tom's case it sounds as though his imagination is training him. What academics frequently regard as virtuous, such as an imagination for the situation of others, the whistleblower often experiences as a burden, an inability to do otherwise. The academic names the virtue, but the whistleblower pays the price.

If whistleblowers are connected in an almost visceral way with the consequences of their acts, this does not mean that they are connected in an almost visceral way with those who are affected by them. Tom's concern for the children who might play in the dust is unusual. Most do not talk about the others they are serving except in the most general terms, such as "the public." In this regard they are different from rescuers.

Consider how Magda Trocmé, a rescuer, spoke about "covering" the Jews she cared for. "When you cover people, you are allowing their own heat to warm their bodies under that blanket or sweater; you are not intruding on those bodies. . . . In this image of covering lies the essence of Magda's way of caring for others" (Hallie 1979, 65). The rescuer makes a mammalian connection with another, a lived attachment to another person, that is lacking for the whistleblower.

Martin Buber (1965, 175) wrote that empathy is like a bridge, thrown "from self-being to self-being across the abyss of dread of the universe." For whistleblowers, one end of this bridge must generally be supported by an imaginary abutment.

This is no small difference. It means that the rescuer is acting in accordance with our mammalian human nature. The rescuer may be going against the larger group, but he or she is forming an attachment with another, perhaps the basic human (actually, mammalian) act (de Waal 1996, 174). It is no accident that rescuers use a lot of skin talk, their relationship with the victim a type of skinship.

One rescuer put it this way: "When I came home, I looked at my skin. You see I looked and I said to myself 'Of course we are the same!' " (Fogelman 1994, 262). Like whistleblowers, rescuers speak in several voices. Unlike whistleblowers, one of these voices is often talking skin talk.

Whistleblowers' loyalties are different, more abstract. They are acting against an aspect of human nature, which tells us something important about "human nature." It too is only one voice, albeit a powerful one. "Regardless of circumstances, chimpanzees, monkeys, and humans cannot readily exit the group to which they belong. The double meaning of 'belonging to' says it all: they are part of and possessed by the group" (de Waal 1996, 169). In such groups, the leading strategy is alliance: two against one. "Many primates excel at this: their main tool for internal competition is the alliance of two parties against a third" (172). Even rescuers employ this strategy, the rescuer and his or her charge against the world. The whistleblower risks less, but he or she generally risks it alone.

One might argue that although whistleblowers are not connected to those they benefit, the structure of their imagination for consequences is nonetheless the structure of all empathy: taking up in one's imagination the place of the other. Certainly this is true, but it is not simply true, as discussed under the third heading, "identification with the victim."

A Sense of the Historical Moment

"It was just my moral bad luck to be there at the right time," said Joe Goshen. "Or should I say the wrong time? Most people are not faced with being asked to lie to the Feds. I knew at that moment I was going to be part of history."

He was, though it was not history that made the newspapers, just another case of Medicare fraud. But it was history nonetheless. It need not have been. Had Joe been unaware of his historical moment, it might have passed him by. He was waiting for it.

"You sound like you were just waiting to pounce," said another whistleblower.

"No, not pounce. Act. I come from a large family, and each of my brothers and sisters made something of themselves. Suddenly I knew it was my turn. It just didn't make me rich."

It cost Joe his job, but he is lucky. So far it has not cost him his house or family. Though he never got his job back, he was vindicated. His boss eventually went to jail.

"What do you mean by moral bad luck?" I asked.

"If any of my brothers or sisters had been in the same situation they'd have done the same thing. But they weren't. It was my bad luck to be the one to have to pay the price."

Joe was asked to lie about how well his organization was serving its disabled clients. He might have talked with me about his clients and their needs. Instead he talked about himself, his moment in history.

Like Tom Delaney, Joe is attached not so much to others as to his acts. His acts are his children. Acts grow up, leave home, live their own lives, get married, and bring forth other acts, but for his acts' children and grandchildren alike the whistleblower is forever responsible. Perhaps whistleblowers' acts are like children in another sense as well, someone to keep them company in the world. Not other people but a chain of acts serves as the bridge across the abyss of dread to which Buber refers.

Identification with the Victim

"I'd been a part of management for years. They were my friends, we watched each other's kids grow up. But when I finally figured out what they . . . no I don't mean they, I mean we. When I finally figured out what we were doing to the poor people who were our clients, I couldn't even go out for a drink with them anymore. Management was my world, I didn't even know our clients' names, but I had to choose. Only it wasn't really a choice, you know, more like an ultimatum I gave myself." So said Janet Morgan.

Anna Freud (1966, 109–21) wrote about "identification with the aggressor." An early stage in the development of conscience, identification with the aggressor occurs not just when we are scared of others but when we cannot bear their censure. We internalize the criticism, but rather than directing it at ourselves we turn it outward, becoming the critic because we cannot bear the criticism. Moral maturity is reached, says Anna Freud, when we become able to turn this criticism back against ourselves.

That's Freud! Sigmund (1961, 83–96) or Anna, it makes little difference. For both, conscience is the aggression we would have visited on others turned back on ourselves. I do not know if this is true, but I have promised not to posit entities and mechanisms as explanations, so I will not pursue the point, introducing it only to note the possibility nowhere discussed by either Freud, "identification with the victim." Only I introduce it not as mechanism but as choiceless choice.

Somewhere along the way we have to choose. When push comes to shove, are we going to throw in our lot with the executioner or the victim? With power or its victims? Joe put it this way: " 'You're part of management now,' they told me. 'You represent the interests of the company.' Maybe so, but it didn't feel that way. I still felt like a kid, like one of the kids who wasn't getting any services."

Hannah Arendt (1997, 237–49) divides the world into parvenus and pariahs. Which shall we choose to be? Shall we assimilate ourselves to authority or to those who suffer its injustice? What if this choice were the basis of all morality?

To be sure, the world is not always divided so starkly. What marks a historical moment is that suddenly it is, and we have to choose, suddenly to find that we have already made the choice a thousand times before in similar, less dramatic situations, even if we did not know it at the time. This is what Iris Murdoch (1970, 67) means when she says that at crucial moments of choice most of the business of choosing is already over. We have chosen by how we have lived our lives up until this point. Then our lives choose for us. Aristotle (*Nicomachean Ethics*, book 2) had a similar idea. He called it character, *ethos*, the term that comes down to us as ethics.

It is the power of the Milgram experiments in obedience to authority to have created a world in which there were only two choices: identification with the aggressor or identification with the victim. In other words, Milgram created a historical moment. Few imagined that when forced to choose so starkly, most would choose to side with the aggressor, even when they could hear the cries of the victim. We don't help because we are terrified of helplessness, a terror that our competitive culture does little to assuage. Perhaps it is fear of being substituted for the victim that leads so many to side with the aggressor, a fear reinforced by the structure of the Milgram experiment itself. Each "teacher" believed he had a fifty-fifty chance of being the victim. There but for the grace of Odds go I.

One of Milgram's subjects, a professor of the Old Testament who refused to deliver the full battery of shocks, could not, it seems, bring himself to disobey. Instead, he switched allegiances, saying that he was now taking his orders from the victim (Milgram 1974, 49). Unable to say no on his own, the professor chooses to obey another authority, one whom he evidently wanted to obey in the first place. Was this a cowardly compromise? Perhaps, but one gives up a lot, making oneself more exposed and vulnerable to power, when one follows the victims of this world. The professor also says that he takes his orders from a higher authority, God. In assimilating God to the victim, he has accomplished some subtle theology.

Until this point I have suggested that whistleblowers are not primarily motivated by empathy, their "skinship," with the victim. Am I not now suggesting they are? Not necessarily. Whistleblowers identify with the victim by making the victim's fight their own. It does not matter that in many cases the whistleblower does not know the actual victim. On the contrary, that just makes it easier. Identification with the victim may be defined not as empathy with the sufferer but as resistance to the aggressor, a refusal to ally oneself with the aggressor, as the quotation from Janet Morgan that opens this section reveals.[2]

This need not be the case. Tom, the whistleblower who speaks about his imagination for consequences, combines empathy with resistance. My point is not logical, or even psycho-logical, but empirical. As most whistleblowers talk about it, their identification with the victim takes the form of a refusal to align themselves with the aggressor, coupled with an inability not to choose sides. In good measure this inability stems from a reluctance or incapacity to double.

Not Very Good at Doubling

"When I came home at night, I was supposed to love and care about my family," said Jane Bryan. "And I did. When I went to work in the morning, I was supposed to regard everyone else's family as expendable. After a while I just couldn't do it anymore."

"Why'd it take you ten years?" asked another whistleblower.

"I don't know. I think I just got used to living in two different worlds. Then somehow I just couldn't anymore."

The whistleblower is not very good at "doubling," as Robert Jay Lifton (1986, 418–29) calls it. Lifton introduced the concept to explain how the Nazi doctors who experimented on Jews could do it. Doubling takes place when a part of the self comes to act autonomously, as though part of the self were authorized to act for the entire self. It is through doubling that we are able to ignore our ethical qualms at work because our work self temporarily speaks for our whole self. Doubling takes place when the voices that speak to us no longer speak to each other, as when the voice of the family self no longer hears the voice of the work self, and vice versa.

One businessman, not a whistleblower, put it this way: "What is right in the corporation is not what is right in a man's home or in his church. What is right in the corporation is what the guy above you wants from you. That's what morality is in the corporation" (Jackall 1988, 6).

The businessman tells a tale in which three selves have trouble talking with each other because they inhabit worlds in which different moral languages are spoken. An implicit master narrator exists, the one who tells the tale of the other isolated narrators, but the master narrator is a shadowy presence. He is an observer, perhaps even a mourner of their lost unity that never was, but he is no integrator. Because a shadowy master narrator is present, one would have to say the man's doubling (actually, tripling) is not complete, though it would be more accurate, and certainly more in accord with Lifton's thinking, to say that he has doubled but not split. The man retains awareness of other selves with other stories, but each is sequestered in a little room, like the subject and his victim in the Milgram experiments.

It would be possible to elaborate the concept of doubling further, as Lifton does, but it does not seem necessary. What is important is that something like doubling seems a requirement of modern life. From Kant to Max Weber to Jürgen Habermas, modern life is defined in terms of its separation into spheres of value, as they are sometimes called: science, religion and morality, and art. Unproblematic, even liberating in the abstract, this division becomes immensely problematic when organization and bureaucracy become one of these spheres, a type of pseudo-science.

This is precisely what the critique of instrumental reason, as the Frankfurt School calls it, is all about, its explanation of the Holocaust. When we think instrumentally, we treat others, as well as ourselves, as things, to whom moral categories do not apply. This is what Habermas's project is concerned with, the colonization of the lifeworld, as he calls it, by strategic and instrumental action. This is what Bauman means when he says all social organization consists of subjecting the conduct of its units to either instrumental or procedural criteria of evaluation. Doubling is a sophisticated emotional and cognitive act, one that whistleblowers are unable or unwilling to perform. In this regard, they are dysfunctional actors in modern society.

A Sense of Shame

Whistleblowers talk about shame a lot, and they talk about it in ways that are often surprising. One whistleblower said that he felt shame at being an employee of an agency that no longer cared about the public. Though not all whistleblowers use the language of shame or guilt, many talk about feeling dirty or corrupted by the acts of others with whom they are associated. Don Bloom put it this way: "I'm ashamed of what my company did, and I'm ashamed that I had to blow the whistle. I'm ashamed for the people I worked with, and I'm ashamed for the people who were hurt by what my company did."

"You did the right thing," I responded. "Why should you feel shame?"

"Because I was part of that world," he said. He does not mean that he contributed to the neglect of his company's clients but that he cannot separate herself from those who did.

Don Bloom's integrity is loose in the world, too loose, it might be argued, affected by too many things he did not do. Those with a psychological cast of mind might wonder about the childhood sources of his

73

shame, but it does not really matter. What matters is that his shame helps him see how truly connected he is to the acts of others. Like it or not, he is part of a fleshy human web that includes its least moral members.

In a chapter titled "Shame," Primo Levi (1988, 70–71) writes that both the inmates of Auschwitz and their Russian liberators felt shame. But the Germans did not.

> It was the same shame which we knew so well, which submerged us after the selections, and every time we had to witness or undergo an outrage: the shame that the Germans never knew, the shame which the just man experiences when confronted by a crime committed by another, and he feels remorse because of its existence, because of its having been irrevocably introduced into the world of existing things, and because his will has proven nonexistent or feeble and was incapable of putting up a good defense.

Whistleblowers talk in remarkably similar terms about how the just man can be shamed by the deeds of the unjust. Statements such as "I just felt so ashamed to be a member of [an organization] that would lie in public" were common. So too were statements such as "I just felt dirty whenever I was at work. I couldn't wait to get home and change." Unjust deeds pollute the world and make us all feel ashamed, especially if we are too weak to do anything to rectify them. Above all, shame is an experience of weakness, and while one might argue that this experience is irrational (even narcissistic, as though one man could defeat the Nazis), it is first of all human. Shame's origins in feelings of doubt and weakness about one's goodness help explain the close relationship between shame and narcissism, as I will argue shortly.

Shame is not a popular concept these days, though a couple of recent books have sought to rehabilitate it (Lasch 1995; Lewis 1992). A standard reading of shame sees it as an immature predecessor of guilt: shame is about what others think of us; guilt is about what we think of ourselves (Benedict 1946, 222–23).

If guilt is about fear of loss of love and protection, as Freud argued, then the distinction need not be so sharply drawn. Guilt is the internalization of this fear, so that we fear love's loss even when others are not about, but this does not make guilt more moral. It may make the guilty one more likely to follow orders when the one who gives the orders is not around. Eichmann disobeyed the orders of his superiors to stop killing Jews because he knew in his heart that Hitler would never have approved (Arendt 1964, 148–49). As Eli Sagan (1988) puts it, the problem with the Nazis is not that they had too little superego but too much.

We should at least consider the possibility that the more social quality of shame is good, connecting us with a world of others, rather than isolating us with our fear of loss of love. A prototypical experience of shame supports this conclusion: the embarrassment members of an audience may feel when a performer does poorly. We feel it because there is a human connection, in this case a type of identification with the victim.

Frank Whitbred is a chemist who worked for a state environmental protection agency. Several times his boss had refused to allow him to testify before a state panel investigating the agency's failure to test the well water of subdivisions located near sites where hazardous materials had been dumped. Eventually he called up a state senator and told him his story. Shortly thereafter Frank was fired. The state civil service commission made his agency take him back, but he was given no work to do and an office that was once a janitor's closet.

In telling his story, Frank mixed the language of moral and chemical pollution in ways that were sometimes hard to follow.

"I just felt so polluted by the whole experience. I felt ashamed to listen to their lies.... Everyone has a right to know what's in their environment. I spoke up for that right. Now my colleagues won't come near me, they're afraid, like I'm contaminated or something." While the cynic might respond that Frank needs to work on his boundaries, we should consider what kind of world we will live in when nobody feels shame for anything. This seems to be how it works, the capacity to feel shame for one's own acts inextricably interwoven with the capacity to feel shame for others'. Instead of being the poor relative of guilt, shame may better be understood as a sense of being human among humans. This would explain how shame for others and shame for self are connected, as we are all connected in a human world. Shame would come about as close to skin talk as whistleblowers are likely to come.

NARCISSISM MORALIZED

Put this way, nothing the whistleblower says contradicts traditional ethical accounts. The whistleblower feels empathy for others, is ashamed at being associated with unethical acts, and acts himself so as not to feel the greater shame of failing to fulfill his own ethical obligations. The trouble is that this is not how it sounds when the whistleblower is talking. It sounds as though the whistleblower is most concerned with his or her ethical purity. Certainly Frank Whitbred talks this way, distressed above all that he is being contaminated by the corruption of others.

It is not just Molly Higgins who says, "I lost my virginity." Many whistleblowers, and not just women, use the phrase. What they seem to mean is that their experience of themselves as good, whole, and pure has been corrupted, and so they feel ashamed. They have lost their illusions, as well as an illusion of themselves as whole and pure. To some that is the most important illusion of all. The illusion is narcissism. Shame is wounded narcissism. To be overcome with shame by the acts of others is to be wounded narcissistically by being associated with corruption. Doubly wounded, as one was too weak to do anything about it.

Narcissism is a psychoanalytic term that has passed into popular discourse. I use it in that way, blending psychoanalytic with popular insight. Though often taken as a pejorative, narcissism is by no means necessarily negative. It all depends on whether the narcissist raises himself to become one with high ideals, what I call narcissism moralized, or whether the narcissist lowers his ideals to meet the frustrated self.

In an early work, "On Narcissism" (1914), Freud assimilated the ego ideal to the superego, what we call conscience. In subsequent work by Freud, the superego comes to represent the disciplinary side of morality, the part of the self that says, "thou shall not." Freud does not write much more about the ego ideal, but what he does say suggests that it becomes the heir of man's primary narcissism (Chasseguet-Smirgel 1984, 76). The ego ideal represents all one would like to be, or at least all the infant would like to be: so dependent on others that their power is an unacknowledged extension of its own, fused and separate at the same time. Primary narcissism has the quality of the nirvana principle, the quality of an oceanic experience, merged with the All while aware only of oneself.

It sounds terribly primitive, and of course it is. But this same narcissism may be expressed in humanity's highest ideals. The way Plato talks about how humans may share in, participate in, partake of, and assimilate themselves to the Ideas is the language of narcissism. Most exalted experiences have this quality of assimilation to an ideal, whether these experiences take place in a concert hall, a lover's bed, a cathedral, or nature. The narcissistic experience of being one with the All is where these experiences gain their emotional power.

According to Freud (1908), we never give up anything; we only exchange one thing for another. "The Freudian concept of the ego ideal follows on directly from this observation. According to this, the ego ideal is a substitute for primary narcissistic perfection, but a substitute from which the ego is separated by a gulf, a split that man is constantly seeking to abolish" (Chasseguet-Smirgel 1984, 4–5).

The question is only how we seek to abolish the gap. Do we idealize the ideal, filling it with the greatest cultural achievements in which we can then share? Or do we fill the ego ideal with our own grandiosity? These are not entirely separate strategies, but they result in vastly separate lives, as separate as those of Martin Luther King and Alcibiades, Gandhi and Hitler.

Filling one's ego ideal with cultural values not only requires the ability to recognize one's imperfection. It also requires the ability to sustain a heightened sense of imperfection, the experience of oneself as an ailing animal, as Freud put it. The more noble the ego ideal, the less adequate is the self who would fuse with it. The ability to tolerate this heightened experience of imperfection, coupled with the recognition that time and work may lessen but never eliminate the gap, is the best definition of the distinction between mature and immature narcissism.

Making money, raising children, becoming an ideologue, becoming a martyr, becoming company president, writing a book, creating a work of art: all these activities frame and form our narcissism. All require a certain maturity, insofar as all require that one must work within frames and forms – that is, within limits – to lessen the gap be-

77

tween ego and ideal. But while all these activities require maturity, all are not narcissism moralized.

Narcissism moralized requires that the content of the ego ideal – that is, one's ideals – become moral. We worship the gods because they are good, says Socrates, not because it is good to worship the gods. If the ego ideal is the avatar of primary narcissism, then it is good to worship at its altar only when the ego ideal is good. The quotation from Saint Augustine that serves as epigraph to this chapter exemplifies this distinction.

One might argue that narcissism is just the motivation, a psychological impulse that may explain ethical action, but is not itself an ethical category. From this perspective, narcissism would be a special type of anger: rage at being rendered less whole and perfect, what psychoanalysts call narcissistic rage. No more terrifying anger exists, in part because it is so implacable.

The argument that narcissism is a special type of anger comes close to the mark, as long as we understand this anger as akin to what Plato (*Republic* 439e–441d) calls thumos: the human spirit that feels indignation at baseness and corruption. Above all, thumos rebels at anything that would bring shame upon the self. The trick is to educate thumos so that it gets shamed by the right things, or should I say the wrong ones? It is not an easy task, says Plato, but it has the advantage of working with nature, not against it.

The late Ron Ridenhour, the soldier who reported the My Lai massacre, exemplified this nature. He was, he said, furious that his buddies would murder innocents. But he was even more enraged at the army brass who put them in the moral morass of Vietnam in the first place. The brass had corrupted his buddies' innocence. Suddenly he was in a whole new world, a world he didn't want to be in, a world in which he would have to act to purify himself of knowledge he had gained but never wanted. That too made him furious. While he felt genuine compassion for the victims at My Lai, their suffering was not, it seems, the deepest source of his anger. That was reserved for those who would corrupt his, and his buddies', innocence.[3]

The narcissistic rage of the whistleblower is in some ways his least attractive aspect. It is, in a sense, utterly selfish: a sense of "Look what you have done to my moral purity!" What distinguishes the whistle-blower's narcissism from that of the ordinary narcissist is that the whistleblower's narcissism is wounded by the right thing: that he was cast into an environment of lies and deception and was expected to become just like everyone else. In a word, the whistleblower's narcissism has become moralized.

One can debate at length whether moral narcissism is admirable. My opinion is that categories like "admirable" are not relevant. Why people act ethically is a far richer and more mysterious phenomenon than we know, and our first category should be wonder, not judgment. What is clear about moral narcissism is its power. Not too many things will make a man or woman give up everything for his or her beliefs, but wounded narcissism is one. Some people will go to the ends of the earth to salve their wounded narcissism, devoting their lives to their moral purification. It is, I believe, the source of the lives of the saints and the lives of not a few sinners and fanatics too.

Whistleblowers act; they blow the whistle. Most people don't act in similar circumstances. This, one might argue, is the salient moral distinction. I am taking the argument one step further. The fact that the whistleblower acts is not something to be explained in addition to the fact that the whistleblower is ethical. If one understands the whistle-blower's experience as one of shame and wounded narcissism, then the act follows by virtue of the character of the experience. Only "follows" is really the wrong word. The act is compelled by the experience, the true meaning of choiceless choice. The sender is the ego ideal.

To be sure, the whistleblower might have dealt with his or her wounded narcissism by other means – inflicting shame on another, for example. But this would not have been narcissism moralized, just narcissism. Once narcissism becomes moralized, the act follows as the day the night, or is it the other way around? Why narcissism becomes moralized as it does is an interesting question but one that I do not wish to answer, for all the reasons discussed in chapter 1. Rather than trying to explain its sources, it will make more sense to wonder at its appearance.

Moral narcissism is not always expressed as rage. More often it is expressed as the idea that the whistleblower is the true organization, though perhaps that too is a type of rage. As one whistleblower put it, "I represented the real [organization]. They said I was disloyal, but they're the real traitors. They forgot who we were working for." He meant the ideas of the organization's founders. It was not the whistleblower who was disloyal to the organization; the organization was disloyal to him. We should not, I have suggested, too quickly equate this position with one in which the whistleblower is loyal to principles over people.

Alcibiades, one of the world's great traitors (as well as one of the world's great narcissists), said much the same thing when he defected from Athens to Sparta, telling Sparta how to win the Peloponnesian War. He was ever, he said, loyal to the true Athens (Thucydides, *History* 6.89–93). It is hard to know how to take this assertion. On the one hand, the Athenians had falsely accused Alcibiades and were preparing to convict him on trumped-up charges. On the other hand, Alcibiades is one of the most selfish characters the world has known, defecting back to Athens and finally to Persia, loyal in the end only to himself.

What makes the difference between Alcibiades and the man or woman of principle is not the absence of narcissism in the latter but what the narcissism is hitched to: the self in all its glory, or the self that so identifies with its ideals that it becomes them. Narcissism becomes moral when the self's commitment to the highest ideals is based in the internalized image of an ideal self, so bound to its ideals that there is in the end no difference between the ideal self and ideals of the self (Kohut 1985). Ironically, narcissism may be the strongest motivator of unselfish behavior – that is, behavior that ignores the interests of the objective, day-to-day self in the world. Narcissism, in other words, may be a particularly demanding sender.

Lawrence Rockwood was an army captain assigned to the United States invasion and occupation of Haiti in 1994, Operation Uphold Democracy. While there he became convinced that his commanding general was failing to protect the human rights of Haitians. Eventually he conducted his own inspection of a Haitian jail, for which he was court-martialed (Shacochis 1999, 143–52).

Rockwood had been raised in a family with a long military tradition. Rockwood men had fought against slavery in the Civil War and against genocide in World War II. Rockwood grew up in Europe, and his father, who had liberated a concentration camp in Czechoslovakia, took young Lawrence to see Dachau. When he was assigned to Haiti, Lawrence was elated. Finally, he thought, he would have his opportunity to liberate an oppressed people. Instead, he was ordered to stay on base and not venture out. The goal, it appears, was to avoid American casualties at all costs.

Rockwood is convinced that in ignoring the horrific situation of Haitians jailed by the paramilitary police, his commanding general was violating the Nuremberg principles, which require that the military protect civilian lives. Rockwood talks as if he is the loyal repository of the true ideals of the military. His commanding general, in contrast, is a traitor to the army and the great military tradition Rockwood's family represents. Rockwood does not believe that only he is loyal to these ideals, but he believes he was justified in disobeying his commander because he knows and remembers what his superiors had forgotten, if they ever really knew. It is hard to say that Rockwood is wrong. Or rather, it is hard to say that his narcissism has not become moralized.[4]

CHAPTER 5

Implications of Whistleblower Ethics for Ethical Theory

The enemies of art and of morals, the enemies that is of love, are the same: social convention and neurosis. – Iris Murdoch, "The Sublime and the Good"

I s the moral narcissism of many whistleblowers just a curious empirical finding, or is it more? Does it challenge conventional accounts of ethics? It depends in part on what one thinks is, and ought to be, the relationship between ethical theory and moral psychology, that department of philosophy under which I will temporarily locate the phenomenon of narcissism moralized.

This should not be a relationship of replacement, as though one had to choose between one or the other.[1] The relationship should be what John Rawls (1971) calls reflective equilibrium, in which we go back and forth between moral psychology and moral theory, using one to illuminate the other. In other words, our moral discourse should leave room for the study of moral practice. The language of moral discourse should remain connected to an analysis of moral life as it is actually lived.

Against this argument, one might claim that it is not the job of moral theory to talk with moral actors. The physicist, a theoretician, uses a special language to describe round objects in motion. The baseball pitcher, a practitioner, uses quite a different vocabulary, such as curve ball, to describe the motion of the round object he throws. That baseball players do not use the language of physics to describe the flight of the baseball does not impugn the language of physics. Similarly, that whistleblowers do not use the language of the categorical imperative says nothing about Kant's moral theory. They belong to different, even incommensurable, universes of discourse.

83

IMPARTIALISM

When I say "Kant's moral theory," I mean not just Kant's but what are often called impartialist moral theories, characterized by principles that represent an impartial point of view (Blum 1994, 14; Darwall 1983). "Do unto others as you would have them do unto you" is an impartialist moral principle.[2] Impartialist moral theory, the most popular theory in the Western world, is concerned with principles, obligations, and duties that are equally binding on all men and women in similar situations (Donagan 1977, 7).

Two questions are raised by the morality of whistleblowers, the morality of narcissism moralized. Is it truly different from the morality of impartialism, the theory of morality in the Western world? If it is, how should this affect our view of impartialism? I will address these questions in turn. The simple answer is that narcissism moralized is different from the morality of impartialism and that we should therefore be troubled by impartialism. But of course it is not this simple.

One might argue that the morality of whistleblowers is entirely compatible with impartialism. One would not expect that whistleblowers would use the language of impartialism. Impartialism is an abstract theory. But the language whistleblowers do use accords with the ethical tradition to which impartialism is related. Consider the five stories that whistleblowers tell: an imagination for consequences, a sense of the historical moment, identification with the victim, not very good at doubling, and shame. Are these not stories about duty, conscience, and loyalty to principle over person, the everyday language version of impartialism? Are the whistleblowers not evoking a familiar ethical tradition, whose philosophical expression is impartialism?[3]

One could interpret what the whistleblowers say in these terms, but one need not. It is not what I heard. To interpret what whistleblowers said in these terms would be more about fitting the tradition, or rather about hearing only what fits the tradition. What I heard were stories in which whistleblowers were loyal not to principles but to ideal selves who embody these principles. It would be wrong to conclude that these ideal selves only happened to embody these principles. The principles are what make them ideal, as the epigraph from Augustine suggests. But the principles obtain value only as they are embodied in oneself. Whatever that is exactly, it is not impartialism.

An imagination for consequences is more about thinking about one's acts as one's children than it is about thinking about the real children who might play in the radioactive dust. It is both, of course, and it would be foolish to say it is one or the other, but it was my impression that most whistleblowers are more attached to their acts than to the people affected by them. It is possible, of course, that this attachment to their acts is a result of having suffered so severely for them; the whistleblowers' original motivation was more other-regarding. It is my impression that for whistleblowers it is a fuzzy distinction in the first place.

A sense of the historical moment certainly involves a sense of one's responsibility to others. Those whistleblowers who invoked it seemed most impressed with their own role in history, both as a source of comfort and as motivation. How this might be related to narcissism is apparent.

Identification with the victim certainly involves a concern for others; the whistleblower's story would make no sense without this concern. But identification with the victim is at least as much about a refusal to identify with the aggressor, who is usually in a position of authority. Identification with the victim is more about resistance than compassion, more about idealizing the role of self as the true organization than skinship with the victim.

Not very good at doubling may be interpreted as not being very good as walling off one's moral principles from the way one lives one's life. It may equally well be interpreted as not very good at living with one's wounded narcissism, not very good at isolating and compartmentalizing the damage to one's moral purity that comes from living every day. Not very good at doubling may mean not very good at living with a chasm between ego and ego ideal.

The relationship of a sense of shame to narcissism is clear. Shame is wounded narcissism. This is not to say that shame is inexplicable in terms of one's failure to live up to moral principles. Nevertheless, the shame many whistleblowers feel is so global, so connected to the failure of others to be moral, so ashamed for the human race, that it seems closer to what Freud called an oceanic feeling, the legacy of narcissism. What many whistleblowers want is for the organization to be good, so they can be elevated, rather than shamed, by participating in it. Who would not want such a thing?

Even admitting all this, one might still argue that the morality of whistleblowers is compatible with impartialism along the following lines. One would not expect that whistleblowers would use the language of impartialism. Impartialism is an abstract theory. The distinction between "ideal" and "ego ideal" is at best an issue in moral psychology, at worst a distinction without a difference. All that matters, the traditional moral theorist would continue to argue, is the content of the ego ideal, not how it gets its content. If the ego ideal is characterized by a commitment to impartiality, then it is moral; if not, then it is not. To say that the whistleblower's narcissism has become moral is to say no more, and no less, than that the whistleblower has idealized and internalized the principles that are our ethical tradition's equivalent of impartiality. That brings us back to traditional ethics.

It is a good argument, but it is not true. How we hold our principles matters, and narcissism moralized means not merely that principle is integrated into the self (when, in fact, it is) but that the principle becomes the self. When principle becomes one with the purity and perfection of the self, so that holding to this principle is the form in which the self's perfection is expressed and contained (which is what narcissism moralized means), then it is no longer a principle in any sense that might be retrieved by ethical impartialism. Almost any other principle, one is tempted to say, but not that one, is compatible with narcissism moralized. Narcissism is not impartialism.

Loyalty provides an interesting way of thinking about the relationship between impartialism and narcissism. Impartialists don't like loyalty because loyalty is particular, not universal. Loyalty concerns what we owe certain individuals or relationships because of our unique history that binds us to them.[4] At least one philosopher has tried to get around this, arguing that we may be loyal to our highest principles (Royce 1971). From this angle, loyalty looks like a species of universalism. This is certainly what whistleblowers say. In fact, it is probably their most popular expression of their fate. "I got fired because I put loyalty to principles over loyalty to my boss." Whistleblowers say this, in part, because they are mortified at the thought of having been disloyal.

Generally I have tried to follow whistleblowers' lead in thinking about these things, but in this case I cannot, or at least not as most whistleblowers would wish to be followed. Not only does it not make sense to talk about loyalty to principles over people, but this distinction would make it possible to ignore the well-being of real people in favor of some abstract principle (Ladd 1967). What sense does it make, for instance, to charge someone with being disloyal to the Constitution, a set of principles? What could it mean? (Fletcher 1993, 63). Certainly not that one disagreed with another about the meaning of a particular clause. That's not disloyalty but a difference in interpretation. And if one did not value the Constitution to begin with, the charge of disloyalty would hardly apply. One may be disloyal to one's country, a group of people, but not to its abstract principles.

Yet whistleblowers are not wrong to talk about their loyalty. I have seldom met men and women as loyal as they. Never have I met men and women as tortured by the thought that they have been disloyal. If loyalty is related to fidelity, as it is, then the whistleblower is loyalty's most faithful servant – faithful, that is, to the whistleblower's ego ideal. In the ego ideal, principle and person become one, and it is to this principled person that whistleblowers are loyal, the best part of themselves, or at least the most demanding.

George Fletcher (1993, 14–15, 83) says that it makes loyalty vacuous to talk about loyalty to oneself. Instead, we are properly loyal only to others with whom we share a history. He calls these others "part of oneself." But isn't this just what the ego ideal is? Fletcher thinks loyalty can't apply to the self because the self is just one thing. But if the self speaks to itself in several voices, then the concept of loyalty to oneself makes perfect sense. Loyalty means that one voice is faithful to another, heeding no other voices, inside or out. Narcissism moralized is an extreme case of faithfulness, in which the whistleblower heeds only the voice of his sender, the ego ideal. It would, I have suggested, be better if the ego ideal were a little more loyal to the material interests of the ego, but that is not how it works with most whistleblowers. They are loyal to a fault, even if this fault is in themselves, the utterly un-compromising voice of the ego ideal.

PARTICULARISM

Impartialism is not the only ethical theory, of course, not even in the Western world. Particularism is a leading contender. Among well-known works of moral particularism are Iris Murdoch's (1970) *The Sovereignty of Good*, Carol Gilligan's (1982) *In a Different Voice*, and Nel Noddings's (1984) *Caring: A Feminist Perspective on Ethics and Education*. Particularism is rooted in our concerned responsiveness to particular individuals. From this per-spective, personal relationships are the principal setting in which moral acts take place. The moral act is not a matter of finding reasons or princi-ples but of getting oneself to pay attention to the reality of other people and their needs (Blum 1994, 12). It is, says Murdoch, a perspective that has been "theorized away" in contemporary ethics.

Although it may have been theorized away, particularism has not been experimented away. On the contrary, a number of psychologists have sought to distinguish particularism from its simulacrum, low-quality altruism. Low-quality altruism, it is said, is expressed in terms of "If I were in your shoes" and is based on mere identification. High-quality altruism is expressed in terms of "imagining I were you" and is based on sympathetic insight into the needs of the other, a perspective that comes close to Murdoch's (Kohn 1990, 232–34).

One might call narcissism moralized "low-quality altruism," ex-cept that it really isn't altruism at all, so it can't be low quality. It is a narcissistic extension of the boundaries of the self, so that the self is shamed by the misdeeds of others. Lest the reader wonder how nar-cissism, a tenet of the self, can be extended, the reader need only think of the way in which parents take pride in their children, almost as if their children were an extension of themselves. Or the way members may take pride in their group, or citizens their nations. The narcissis-tic ego is like the amoeba, eager to extend its pseudopod to absorb others in the interests of the ideal self, above all its goodness.

Extension may involve a disrespect of the integrity of others, but it need not. Not every parent who identifies with the fate of his or her child disrespects the child's individuality, but some do. One measure of narcissism moralized is the degree to which it can respect the existence of independent others. Indeed, this is how mature narcissism is best defined: that it uses the frame and form of difference for its projects. This respect for difference, though, is still not the particularity that Murdoch and Gilligan are talking about. The reality of the particular other is not the moral polestar. That remains the ego ideal, avatar of narcissism, the self fused with its ideals, including ideas and others.

The whistleblower, it is apparent, comes no closer to the particularist than the impartialist. To be sure, the whistleblower is concerned with the suffering of others. But this is not what leads the whistleblower to act. The whistleblower acts because the unjust suffering of others leads the whistleblower to feel morally corrupted by association. The whistleblower's boundaries are permeable; they include others but not particular others. Or at least it is not their particularity that motivates the whistleblower. If the whistleblower is not loyal to principle over person, neither is she loyal to person over principle, unless, that is, the person is his or her own ideal self.

VIRTUE ETHICS

Could whistleblower ethics be a version of virtue ethics, as it is called, the ethics of human excellence? From the perspective of virtue ethics, the key question is not "What ought I to do?," but "What kind of person should I be?" Isn't this precisely what whistleblowers are concerned with, the excellence of their selves? Conversely, isn't the shame felt by whistleblowers much like the shame that motivates the virtuous Greek to excellence?

Socrates (*Gorgias* 482c) does not sound like a whistleblower when he says it would be better for me "that my lyre or chorus I directed should be out of tune and that multitudes of men should disagree with me than that I, being one, should be out of harmony with myself, and contradict me." If I inflict an injustice, I must live with the unjust one forever. If I suffer an injustice, I need only live with the consequences of another's injustice.

But while whistleblowers do not sound like Socrates, the reasoning is similar. Like Socrates, it is the dread of having to live forever with someone whom one despises that motivates the whistleblower. No narcissistic injury is more profound than that. Indeed, this dread could be said to define narcissism: that one will be scorned by one's ego ideal. *Whistleblowers blow the whistle because they dread living with a corrupted self more than they dread isolation from others.* It is as simple and complicated as that. Is this not Socrates' motivation as well?

It was Jane Bryan's inability not to talk with herself about what she was doing that led her to blow the whistle, though perhaps the term "compelled" would be more accurate. Certainly that is how she experiences her life. The difference, it is worth remembering, is that Socrates' little voice, his *daemon*, kept him out of trouble for seventy years by telling him not to get involved in politics, for he would get himself killed. The whistleblower's daemon, his sender (for that is what the daemon is), is more demanding. Unlike Socrates' daemon, the whistleblower's demands action.

Some argue that Socrates' conscience is troublingly selfish—that is, troublingly narcissistic (Kateb 1984, 101–3). Socrates is unconcerned with the suffering of others and the injustice inflicted on them. He wants only not to be involved so he can remain a friend to himself. This is consistent with what we know of Socrates' ethical disobedience from *The Apology*. Socrates twice refused to participate in illegal acts by withdrawing from politics. He just went home, presumably to talk with himself.

George Kateb (1984, 102) sees the same deficiency in Hannah Arendt's discussion of those few who refused collaboration with the Nazis, even at the risk of their lives. "She says that their refusal stemmed from their fear of self-abhorrence. Although in that context, she does not suggest anything but admiration for their refusal, she nevertheless diminishes their heroism by concentrating so exclusively on their inner dialogue. She does not depict them as overcome by horror at the wrong done others." Kateb expresses a view of morality that finds in the complexity of the moral person not an inspiration to curiosity (how does morality really work?) but only a disappointing impurity. Morality must be other-regarding or it is not really morality.[5]

Kateb may be mistaken, but it is actually Arendt (1978b, part 1, 190) who makes the first mistake, assimilating Socrates' inner dialogue to conscience. More likely it is Socrates' narcissism talking, his rage at being asked to corrupt himself in order to be a citizen of Athens. In psychoanalytic language, Arendt attributes Socrates' voice to his superego, which speaks the language of prohibition, the legacy of the Oedipus complex: "Thou shalt not."

Arendt should have attributed Socrates' voice, his daemon, his guardian spirit, to his ego ideal, which speaks the language of perfection of the self, including moral perfection. Certainly this fits what we know about Socrates from Plato (but of course it is always Plato's Socrates), whose life's work was to convince people that their happiness and goodness depend on no one but themselves.

"Thought" is the term Arendt gives to Socrates' inner dialogue, his conversation with himself. It is Arendt's almost desperate hope that a thoughtful person's ability to be dissatisfied with the self he or she is living with, as Jane Bryan was, might serve as an antidote to evil and a source of goodness. During what Arendt calls "boundary situations" and "special emergencies," the internal dialogue becomes impossible to continue unless the thoughtful one acts in the world to bring the selves back into a friendly relationship.[6] One does this, says Arendt, by saying no.

By "boundary situation," Arendt (1978b, part 1, 192) means something similar to what I mean by a sense of the historical moment. It is an experience of "something immanent which already points to transcendence, and which, if we respond to it, will result in our '*becoming the Existenz we potentially are.*' "[7] Is this not the philosophical language version of becoming one with one's ego ideal?

Earlier I adopted Arendt's view of thought as my definition of individuality. Individuality means talking with oneself about what one is doing in a spirit serious enough that it might make a difference in what one does. Consequently, I'm tempted to just go along with her here, but I cannot. While Arendt captures the spirit of immanent resistance that marks the whistleblower, she is mistaken to attribute this resistance to thought. She says, "If there is anything in thinking that can prevent men from doing evil, it must be some property inherent in the activity itself, regardless of its objects" (Arendt 1978b, part 1, 180; also p. 5). Why? So thought can reclaim a little something of the great spirit of Reason?[8]

Not only is thinking far more frequently implicated in self-deception than Arendt recognizes, but thinking isn't powerful enough even in her own account. Thinking sounds a little too much like that grand and glorious Reason (*Vernuft*) that has so often gotten Continental philosophy in trouble, as though reason could do anything on its own. Not thinking but the self-revulsion that stems from having failed to live up to high ideals, the self-revulsion that so often takes the form of feeling corrupted by others' misdeeds, is the motive force. Thinking only (and it is a big "only") makes this feeling more available.

"Socratic two-in-one heals the solitariness of thought," says Arendt (1978b, part 1, 187). By this she means that in talking to oneself one brings the parts into conversation, so that the self is not so lonely. It is a nice story, but it is not how it works, at least as far as ethical resistance is concerned. In thinking (what I have called not very good at doubling), the whistleblower becomes aware of the terrible gulf between the ego ideal and the real. It is this gulf, this terrible separation from the narcissistic experience of wholeness, that the narcissist cannot stand.

The mature narcissist acts to bridge the gulf by becoming his ideals, ideals that recognize the separateness of others and the imperfection of the world. One might argue that this too is a type of conversation. I would argue that it is so much more and perhaps so much less as well: not conversation, but fusion with an ideal, made necessary by the dread of moving ever further from it – that is, away from the *Existenz* we potentially are.

Thinking is better seen as a distinct variety of internal conversation, one that fosters a dialogue between sender and subject (ego ideal and ego), so that their relationship is not a totalitarian affair. A strong sender is better than no sender at all, but a strong sender not only cares nothing for its subject but is always at risk of arrogance, such as the secret belief that "I am the true organization."

"Are you sure?" the subject might reply, and they could take the dialogue from there. Thinking performs much the same function as democracy, bringing other voices into the mix and so tempering the extremes. This is why, of course, we often think best in the company of others, who add their real voices to the mix. If, that is, these others are able to hear.

I began this section by wondering if narcissism moralized is an instance of virtue ethics. Certainly they have much in common. For both the goodness of the self is the highest value. Becoming the existence we potentially are is not only a good interpretation of the narcissistic ideal; it is a good interpretation of excellence. If, that is, this existence is good. Moralized narcissism does not abandon standards and principles. It just locates them in the ego ideal, making hash of categories such as impartiality or particularity. This is not the same as reducing standards and principles to the level of the self. That is immature narcissism, narcissism immoralized.

If narcissism moralized is compatible with true excellence, it still seems wrong to equate it with virtue ethics. Certainly narcissism moralized can help us answer the leading questions of virtue ethics, such as "What is a good man like?" and "Can he or she be fostered?" To find a better answer to the latter question is the best reason to integrate moral psychology into moral theory. Nevertheless, there is no reason to assume that narcissism moralized is the only, or even the main, source of ethical action. It is, likely, one of several sources. It is particularly valuable in those cases in which the costs of ethical action are likely to be loss of station and status, one's place in the world. For narcissism moralized provides a quite literally self-ish motive for people to sacrifice the apparently objective interests of the self.

While narcissism moralized is a source of excellence, there is no reason to equate it with human excellence per se, and that in the end is what the ethics of *arete* are about. On the contrary, one of the dangers of narcissism moralized is that moral ideals will come to follow the ideal of narcissistic perfection, rather than setting its standards. Socrates didn't see that as a problem. The perfect self of the just man would naturally be virtuous in all the conventional – that is, social – senses as well. About that we should be skeptical, which is why we should resist the equation of narcissism moralized with human excellence.

Moral theory can and should assimilate moral psychology, but they are not one. Like that other gulf between moral theory and practice, the gulf between moral theory and moral psychology has its virtues. As if truth were proven by the continued existence of man, said Nietzsche in a moment of great insight. As if morality were proven by whatever satisfies the mature narcissist. Not even reflective equilibrium can make them one, and it should not try. The goal is that moral psychology and moral theory converse. Talking with those who have acted ethically about why they did so is a way of beginning this conversation, not ending it.

CONCLUSION

Why assume that everyone who acts morally acts for the same reasons, or should? Certainly whistleblowers seem less particularistic than rescuers of Jews during the Holocaust.[9] But perhaps rescuers are especially connected. Certainly rescuers use a lot of skin talk. Whether whistleblowers are different, and how different they are, is an interesting question because it suggests the possibility that morality is more narcissistic than we know. That is, morality is neither impartial nor particularistic. Morality is narcissistic, concerned to preserve the moral purity of the self. From this perspective, the question becomes not whether but how the self involves others in the project of its moral perfection.

Lawrence Blum (1994, 65–97) distinguishes between Ed Corcoran, who while taking no risks cared for his emotionally ill wife with great decency for years, and Oscar Schindler, who took enormous risks to save hundreds of Jews while treating his wife poorly. He compares both to John Sassal, a doctor who received great satisfaction, and no less social approval and reward, for serving a poor community. Blum asks, What reason is there to believe that the moral virtues are one? What reason is there to assume that what it takes to be a Corcoran has much to do with being a Schindler? Or a whistleblower?

The whistleblower's battlefield is, it seems, ideally suited to his moral psychology. Not only does the whistleblower have few allies, but the whistleblower generally finds little support from those in whose name he or she is speaking because they are generally anonymous, or at least far removed from the whistleblower's field of battle, the depths of the organization. In place of allies, the whistleblower has ideas: his acts are his children; her moment in history is a source of inspiration and comfort; and his shame over the corruption of the organization is an inspiration for the whistleblower to separate himself from it by blowing the whistle. What marks these ideas is how concrete, even embodied they are. Not "the idea of justice," but "my love child the act," comes closer to the mark.

The whistleblower, it seems, exemplifies Darwin's *Origin of Species*. The whistleblower is a unique character whose moral narcissism is well adapted to the alienation and isolation imposed by his particular moral environment, in which doing right means going it alone. Well adapted to what it takes to blow the whistle, a type of idealism-cum-narcissism, whistleblowers are not so well adapted to what it takes to survive blowing the whistle, a type of cynicism-cum-narcissism. It is why they have such a hard time in the years that follow.

Whistleblowers could be unusual. It could also be true that whistleblowers come closer to the main than we know. Could wounded moral narcissism, the raging fear that we have been morally contaminated by injustice, be the ground of all morality? Or just some? In the last analysis, is our deepest loyalty always to our ideal selves?

Here is what I suspect. Morality stems from empathy, in which we are deeply affected by the sufferings of others. Rousseau (1964) calls it pity (pitié), making it the foundation of all morality. It is easy to feel empathy for the sufferings of others, even when fear and ideology often team up to muffle this feeling. What is difficult is to put one's life, or livelihood, on the line for the sake of others, especially abstract others, with whom one feels empathy. This takes more than empathy. This takes narcissism moralized.

In a sense, morality is easy, if by morality we mean feeling empathy and concern for others. What is so difficult is acting on this basis when the self must pay a terrible price: not just the loss of a job but the loss of one's connection to the world, an experience I have summarized with the term "space-walking." To risk this takes something more than empathy. It takes narcissism.

Whether this is true will require further study, and that is really my point. This study will look roughly like what my study of whistleblowers looks like: an inquiry that seeks out men and women who have acted ethically in different situations in order to see what they have in common and what they do not. This will mean listening carefully to what ethical actors say. This is not, needless to say, the same thing as investigating the social psychological correlates of ethical behavior.

It is possible, indeed easy, to define morality in such a way that listening is unnecessary, the moral psychology of the whistleblower irrelevant. Morality is prescriptive, not descriptive, would be a simple way to do it. The argument that the baseball player has little to teach the physicist, to refer to a previous analogy, is a more sophisticated version of this claim, asserting the incommensurability of metaethics with ethical practice and the language of ethical traditions. One might even make of this incommensurability a moral principle in itself, lest ethical theory lose its capacity for independent judgment, as though judging were more important than understanding.

One could do all these things, but one need not. And if one does, one should at least ask oneself, Why? If part of the reason were to protect the goodness and purity of one's ethical theory, would this not itself be evidence against one's decision? Would this not itself be the shadow of narcissism moralized at the heart of ethics?

CHAPTER 6

Organized Thoughtlessness

All social organization consists therefore in neutralizing the disruptive and deregulating impact of moral behaviour. – Zygmunt Bauman, *Modernity and the Holocaust*

T HE whistleblower is a political actor in a nonpolitical world. This world is called the organization. Everything politically important about whistleblowers and whistleblowing follows from this. It follows, but it does not fit into the usual political categories. In spite of having lived in the modern world for several centuries now, we still have no category for what I call the organization, an entity that is neither society nor bureaucracy nor what Michel Foucault calls a regime of truth, though it shares much with each.

If the whistleblower is a political actor in a nonpolitical world called the organization, it will help to define the organization. I do so from two perspectives: from outside the organization in and from inside the organization out. I emphasize the latter perspective, for it is the perspective not of the social theorist but of Orwell's last man.

Much political theory is today written from the perspective of the margins, which is rightly held to be the most insightful place to be. But the margin in question is almost always occupied by a beleaguered group, not an individual. Or if it is occupied by an individual, it is generally any or every individual, such as the endangered individual, or the mythical individual who is said by the naive to exist but really doesn't. In this chapter and the next, I am going to write political theory from the perspective of particular individuals, whistleblowers whose marginalization is as material as it is abstract. What would political theory look like from the perspective of one who has been pushed not just out of the organization but halfway out of society, ending up with no career, no savings, no house, and no family? What would political theory look like to Al Ripskis, a whistleblower who says, "It's a hell of a commentary on our contemporary society when you must be ready to become an insolvent pariah if you want to live up to your own ethical standards" (Glazer and Glazer 1989, 207). This chapter and the next are that commentary.

THE ORGANIZATION FROM OUTSIDE IN

By the term "organization" I mean an entity as general and ubiquitous as the bureaucracy described by Max Weber (1946, 196–244). I do not call it a bureaucracy because bureaucracy is its own environment, co-extensive with the modern world, even as Weber found it first in ancient China. The organization is a bureaucracy obsessed with its boundaries. In the language of Michel Foucault, the organization is a regime of truth obsessed with the untruth with which it is surrounded. I segue from Weber to Foucault so readily because I am not concerned with the locus of power or its path. Much of the rest of the chapter, and all of the next, are concerned with these issues. Here I am concerned only with the goal of power. Its goal is autarky.

The organization acts as if it lives in a perfectly Hobbesian world: the goal is autarky, and it is achieved via transgression. The organization secures its boundaries only by transgressing the boundaries of others, lest it be transgressed against. In this regard it is misleading to suggest that the whistleblower sets truth against loyalty. This suggests an image of the organization that is too passive and static. The real opposition is between individual and collective transgression. Will the individual be available for the act of collective transgression or will he not?

This, I take it, is an implication of that strain of social theory that runs from Nietzsche through Foucault. Transgression is the normal state of affairs, the force that makes the world go around. It is why, says the wise Diodotus, the Athenians should not destroy the Mytilenians. In rebelling they were only doing what comes naturally (Thucydides, *History*, 3.44–46; Orwin 1994, 156).

It is in this vein that we should read Bauman's (1989, 213–15) statement that all social organization consists in subjecting the conduct of its units to either instrumental or procedural criteria of evaluation. More importantly still, it consists in delegalizing all other criteria, and first and foremost such standards as may render behaviour of units resilient to uniformizing pressures and thus autonomous vis-à-vis the collective purpose of the organization (which, from the organizational point of view, makes them unpredictable and potentially de-stabilizing).

The units Bauman is talking about are people. They are treated as things so that they might be constantly and reliably available for the act of collective transgression, the point of the epigraph that opens this chapter.

Where I differ from Bauman is in emphasizing that the society is not one organization but many. With the term "organization" I emphasize the experience of those inside the organization, and key to this experience is the sense of operating in a hostile environment made up of other organizations. The consequence, says Pat Schroeder, is that most organizations take a "rumps together and horns out" approach (Clark 1997, 1061). It is a telling image, a group of potential scapegoats fused at the hip, as if the only choice in this world were to band with other scapegoats or become one.

In such a world, the most terrifying thought is that representatives of the outside are on the inside, traitors in our midst. The whistleblower becomes an insidious disease, a boundary violator. The former president of General Motors, James Roche, expressed this fear when he said, "Some of the enemies of business now encourage an employee to be disloyal to the enterprise. They want to create suspicion and disharmony, and pry into the proprietary interest of the business. However this is labeled – industrial espionage, whistleblowing or professional responsibility – it is another tactic for spreading disunity and creating conflict" (Clark 1997, 1071).

One may read Roche not so much as confirming Bauman as restating his thesis in the language of everyday organizational paranoia. Against organizational paranoia organizational autarky is the preferred solution: total control of the internal environment to combat the threat from the external environment.[1] Most threatening of all, evidently, is the thought that the proprietary organization isn't really private.

THE ORGANIZATION FROM INSIDE OUT

From the whistleblower's perspective, the bird's-eye view of the social theorist may be quite irrelevant, even misleading. From the whistle-blower's perspective, organizations are particularistic. The organization is organized around men and women called bosses. One serves not an organization and not a purpose. One serves a boss. Organizations are, in other words, based on the principle of vassalage.

A story will help make the point. It is told by Kermit Vandivier (1979), who worked for B. F. Goodrich when it was awarded the contract to manufacture brake assemblies for a new plane being built by LTV Aerospace.[2] Brown, who designed the brake to be as light as possible, could never get it to work right. In every test, no matter how unrealistic, the brake burned up. It was too light; it had too few disks. Working under a tight deadline, Brown told his assistant to fudge the tests, which included intentionally miscalibrating the test instruments. Vandivier worked in the test lab, and he told his lab supervisor about it, a man named Daily. Daily went to a man named Lasch, who was Brown's supervisor. Eventually Lasch ordered Daily, the lab supervisor, to make sure the brake passed the tests, no matter what.

Vandivier went along with the fudged tests, but when the brake was delivered to the air force he got scared, fearing he would be both morally and legally liable if anything happened. So Vandivier went to the FBI, which told him to report to them while continuing to collect information on the inside. There was not much more information to collect. Within weeks the jet almost ran off the runway when the test pilot applied the brakes. The FBI investigated, congressional hearings were held, and both the air force and the Government Accounting Office declared that the brake was dangerous and had not been tested properly.

Testifying before a congressional committee, R. G. Jeter, vice-president and general counsel from company headquarters in Akron, said, "We have thirty-odd engineers at this plant ... and I say to you that it is incredible that these men would stand idly by and see reports changed or falsified.... Just nobody does that."

There may have been thirty-odd engineers in the plant, and B. F. Goodrich may be a major American corporation, with operations in a dozen states and as many foreign countries. But from Vandivier's perspective, the organization was just a few men: Brown, who designed the brake; Jones, Brown's assistant; Lasch, Brown's supervisor; Daily, Vandivier's supervisor and director of the lab; and Strong, Lasch's supervisor. Strong and Lasch may have been under pressure from above, but there is no record to suggest that anyone above Strong's level, and perhaps not even Strong, put pressure on the lab to falsify the tests. The only pressure was to deliver the brake on time.

For all practical purposes (take this phrase literally), Vandivier did not work for B. F. Goodrich. He worked for Daily and Lasch. They hired him, they told him what to do, and eventually Strong fired him after learning that Vandivier went to the FBI. Lasch and Strong were eventually promoted.

One might explain Vandivier's experience in terms of a corporate culture that tolerated shoddy practices and promoted insecure leaders. But like most explanations invoking culture, this explanation would be little more than a redescription of the event using the term "culture."

It would be more helpful to state that Vandivier lived in a feudal world. As one whistleblower put it, "When you work for the agency, you don't serve the agency, you serve your boss. For all practical purposes, it's his fiefdom." It is a common perspective among whistleblowers, and the only question is how to take it – as the limited insight of the last man or as a theoretical contribution. I take it as both.

The organization is more feudal than we know. Power is decentralized, and power is personal, located in the figure of the boss. To be sure, many organizations provide access to the central government of the organization, as it might be called. Even if appeals to this level are likely to get the whistleblower fired, this access still demonstrates that organizations are not feudal but bureaucratic. Or does it?

The second stage of feudalism (which flourished in the thirteenth century) also allowed such appeals. "The central government in some cases deals directly with rear-vassals instead of passing orders down a long chain of command. Royal law-courts play a great role in this reorganization" (Strayer 1965, 19). What marks feudalism is not that there is no appeal. Nor does anarchy mark feudalism. There is nothing anarchic about feudalism. What marks feudalism is that power is a private possession. What that means in the organization today is codified by Robert Jackall (1988, 109–10).

> (1) You never go around your boss. (2) You tell your boss what he wants to hear, even when your boss claims that he wants dissenting views. (3) If your boss wants something dropped, you drop it. (4) You are sensitive to your boss's wishes so that you anticipate what he wants; you don't force him, in other words, to act as boss. (5) Your job is not to report something that your boss does not want reported, but rather to cover it up. You do what your job requires, and you keep your mouth shut.

One can see the privacy of power illustrated in that evidently least feudal of organizations, the United States Army. Captain Lawrence Rockwood, the intelligence officer assigned to Operation Uphold Democracy in Haiti, was eventually court-martialed and convicted of disobeying a lawful order of his commander. His case is on appeal, but his argument was not without resonance in the United States Army. David Meade, the general against whom he made his complaint, retired early, and Richard Potter, the general who replaced Meade not only immediately cleaned out the jails but refused to testify against Rockwood at his trial. *The Immaculate Invasion*, a book about the United States in Haiti, concludes Rockwood's story this way: "Under Potter's command, Captain Rockwood would have been performing his duty. Under Meade's command, Rockwood was a criminal" (Shacochis 1999, 151).

The United States Army is hardly a feudal organization, but it enforces its laws in ways that are entirely compatible with islands of private power – that is, fiefdom. It is, of course, a metaphor to suggest that either Vandivier or Rockwood lived in a feudal world. But then again, feudalism was always metaphor. No one living in what we today called feudal societies ever used the term (Strayer and Coulborn 1965, 3). Feudalism is a high-level abstraction, not a form of government, but characteristic of a society in which political power is not just decentralized but personal rather than institutional. To say that the whistleblower experiences his or her world as feudal is to point out that this is how power looks from the bottom up.

The bottom up is not the only perspective, and I am not suggesting we take it out of sympathy. We should take it into account because it better explains why organizations act as they do. It would be ideal if one could combine top-down and bottom-up perspectives, and the ideal of organizational autarky suggests how this might be done. The organization *is* the vulnerability of its members to the boss. Not for the sake of the boss, but for the sake of the autonomy of the organization, which the boss is charged with representing. For the sake of organizational autonomy, the boss is empowered to sacrifice any individual for any reason, including personal ones.

The result is an organizational atmosphere, a "culture," in which private caprice serves organizational ends, somewhat like the cunning of reason that Hegel wrote of. Perhaps Adam Smith's invisible hand would be a more felicitous metaphor. The caprice of bosses serves the goal of Weberian rationalization and Foucauldian discipline more effectively than any plan. It does so only, however, if the boss keeps his caprice within limits, but this too is compatible with the principle of vassalage.

While the integration of top-down and bottom-up perspectives is satisfying for those of us who admire symmetry, it is practically unimportant and may result in rendering the organization more coherent than it really is. For practical purposes, all that is necessary is that we remember that the organization is not just abstract power but a personal fiefdom. These practical purposes include not just explaining whistleblowing but explaining the way in which the organization deals with ethical resistance in its midst. While much of what the whistleblower experiences has the quality of Foucauldian discipline, it is important to recognize how this discipline serves old-fashioned political power, not just sovereign but feudal.

CONSTRUCTION AND DISCIPLINE OF THE WHISTLEBLOWER

"All people need is a civics lesson," says Ralph Nader. He is responding to those who say we need a new political theory to explain the fate of the whistleblower. If Nader is correct, the civics lesson we require is like nothing anyone ever learned in high school.

What would a civics lesson from Michel Foucault look like? The power that disciplines the whistleblower, he might say, has less to do with the organization's ability to fire the whistleblower than one might suppose. That is merely power's most obvious expression, its last and most visible eruption. Power works in more intimate and subtle ways in the modern world, isolating the insubordinate one from his or her fellows by diagnosing him or her as abnormal or disturbed. Foucault calls this disciplinary power, which casts the gaze of the entire organization on the whistleblower almost as though the organization were a physician, treating the whistleblower not as someone who has challenged the power of the organization but as one who is sick, ill, morally suspect, criminal, or disturbed, and so must be isolated from those who are normal.[3]

Disciplinary power makes of the whistleblower a patient, though we have to understand that term in its broadest sense: one whose flawed perceptions of reality are the result of a moral or emotional illness and who must be reformed by power, lest his symptoms prove catching.

> "You are a slow learner, Winston," said O'Brien gently.
> "How can I help it?" he blubbered. "How can I help seeing what is in front of my eyes. Two and two are four."
> "Sometimes, Winston. Sometimes they are five.... You must try harder. It is not easy to become sane.... Shall I tell you why we have brought you here? To cure you!... We do not merely destroy our enemies: we change them" (Orwell 1949, 209).

Under discipline there can be no political or ethical discourse. Any talking that takes place with the patient is strictly instrumental, aimed at controlling the patient through categorization and labeling. Ideally the patient accepts the label.

"The psychiatrist they sent me to said I was suffering from a histrionic personality disorder," said one whistleblower. "I think that meant I needed to show off. No one else but a show-off would have gone to talk with that environmental group about what we were doing. Well, you know what. I believed them. I really did. For years I believed them ... sometimes I still do. A little bit, sometimes, when I'm feeling bad."

"Nuts and sluts" is what many whistleblowers call this familiar strategy, by which their claims are ignored by finding them to be emotionally disturbed or morally suspect. Anita Hill is the most famous nut and slut in recent years. David Brock (1993) called her that in *The Real Anita Hill: The Untold Story,* a hatchet job that he has since recanted, at least in part.[4] Daniel Ellsberg might have been neutralized in this way had Nixon's plumbers not bungled their burglary of Ellsberg's psychiatrist's office.

In high-stakes court cases it is common for the organization's lawyers to hire private detectives to research every aspect of a whistle-blower's life. Today few records are unavailable. Until a few years ago, the easiest way to get rid of a federal employee was to send him or her to a government psychologist who would find him or her psychologically unfit for duty. The whistleblower psychologist who lives down the street from me had this as his assignment until he blew the whistle on the practice and lost his job. Some whistleblowers report that Employee Assistance Programs, which provide a therapist paid for by the organization, have taken over this disciplinary function.

Of all the things that make whistleblowers crazy, the most maddening is the unwillingness of the organization to listen to them. To listen would be to recognize the whistleblower as an individual with a political or ethical claim on the organization. To listen would be to recognize the whistleblower as a political actor, not a patient. It is this that must be denied in the first place, and it is this that disciplinary power aims at: the transformation of actors into patients and politics into discipline.

Disciplinary power aims to make ethical discourse impossible. "I told them they didn't need to fire me. I'd quit. I had my letter of resignation in my hand. All they had to do was listen to what I had to say and see my evidence. I'd have cleaned out my cubicle that afternoon. But they refused to listen. No one would even talk with me about it. They wouldn't talk with me period. It took them three years to get rid of me. And they're still paying for it."

Rather than listen to Tim Fuchs, his company paid him off with a bonus and early retirement, even if it took the threat of a lawsuit to get them to do it. It was my impression that Fuchs would have sacrificed the money in a minute in order to be heard, but when I asked him he only smiled. Probably that was my idealization.

The discipline that Foucault writes about works through expert knowledge, the knowledge that can diagnose a political protest as an expression of illness or a concern with ethics as a sign of emotional immaturity and maladaptation. In a word, discipline works through diagnosis. Though this diagnosis is often psychiatric or moral, it may also be judicial, as in "you do not have standing to sue, as your act does not fall under the purview of legally protected behavior." Sometimes diagnosis is bureaucratic. "That is not your department and hence not your proper concern." At its heart, diagnosis is concerned with the discipline of categories, under which people and things are classified so that they may be subject to expert knowledge. Experts do not talk with their subjects; they diagnose them, even when the diagnostic language is judicial or bureaucratic or social scientific.

If this is so, then those who write about whistleblowers must be especially careful not to discipline whistleblowers in the guise of studying them. Even sympathetic social scientific studies of whistleblowers and other deviants perform this disciplinary function, making "who" more important than what happened to the whistleblower and what this tells us about the sins of our tribe. Bauman makes much the same point when he argues that if rescuers could have been predicted by social scientific categories, they would not have been rescuers in the first place.

To call it "whistleblower behavior," as several journal articles do, is already to have disciplined the whistleblower, transforming an existential and ethical act into another piece of behavior that may be analyzed and explained by social science. And how does one blow the whistle on social science? That, I take it, is what Foucault and Bauman are trying to do, showing the way it contributes to the normalization of those it studies.

An interesting question is the relationship of disciplinary power to ordinary political power, *arche*: the power to rule. Further complicating this question is my suggestion that the political power faced by the whistleblower has the quality of feudal power. This too is arche – political power wielded as a personal possession.

Foucault's position is that disciplinary power is a new type of power, one that operates in the smallest spaces, where the individual confronts not powerful institutions or individuals but discipline. Capillary power Foucault calls it, power that reaches into individuals so deeply that it makes them who they are.

Capillary power suggests something else as well for Foucault, the way power migrates from the margins of society to the center, like blood returning to the heart. The techniques of discipline that have proven so effective against whistleblowers were first developed in clinics, asylums, prisons, research institutes, and universities, migrating to the rest of society so subtly that we do not even recognize them as practices of power. Instead, we think they are knowledge. It is this that differentiates Foucault's account of power from that of Max Weber, for whom power cascades from top to bottom, if I may mix my metaphors.

In one way or another, the rest of this chapter, and all of the next, are concerned with which account of power is correct: Foucault's, Weber's, or my own, what might be called feudal power. In fact, they are not separate, as the quotation from *Nineteen Eighty-Four* suggests. O'Brien is not, after all, a doctor, but a torturer for a rather old-fashioned totalitarian regime, which hardly needs, or wants, to disguise its power to rule. The discipline to which it subjects Winston Smith and others is a supplement to its brutal regime, not a substitute.

What about feudal power? the reader may be asking. If O'Brien is a totalitarian functionary, then he is hardly lord or vassal. True enough, but the relationship between O'Brien and Winston Smith is intensely personal, more intimate than love (Orwell 1949, 208). One might argue that this is just the victim's misapprehension. I think that it is the victim's insight.

This does not mean that Foucault's account is mistaken, only that it is easy to exaggerate the newness or uniqueness of disciplinary power, just as it would be easy to exaggerate the obsolescence of feudal power. Most important in understanding the situation of the whistleblower is not the nature of the power he or she confronts but the goal that it serves: the sacrifice of the whistleblower, the most venerable goal around.

THE LAW

Hundreds of laws protect whistleblowers. Here are a random dozen (Reynolds 1998, 64–70).[5]

– Civil Service Reform Act of 1978 makes retaliation for whistle-blowing unlawful for "disclosure of information which the employee reasonably believes evidences" fraud, waste, or abuse of authority.

– Clean Air Act Amendments of 1977 prohibit discharging or discriminating against an employee who reports a violation of clean air law.

– Defense Contractor Employee Protection from Reprisal Act of 1986.

– Energy Reorganization Act of 1974 prohibits discharging or discriminating against an employee who reports a violation of nuclear safety.

– Fair Labor Standards Act of 1938 prohibits discharging or discriminating against an employee who reports a violation of child labor or wage and hour laws.

– Financial Institutions Reform, Recovery, and Enforcement Act of 1989 prohibits discharging or discriminating against an employee of a federally chartered credit union or a federally insured depository respectively who reports a violation of audit laws.

– Foreign Service Act of 1980 bars taking any action against a Foreign Service member for disclosing information to Congress.

– Federal [Coal] Mine Safety and Health Act of 1977 prohibits discharging or discriminating against an employee who reports a coal mine violation.

– Occupational Safety and Health Act of 1970 prohibits discharging or discriminating against an employee who reports a violation.

– Labor Management Relations Act of 1947 prohibits discharging or discriminating against an employee who reports a violation.

– Surface Transportation Assistance Act of 1982 prohibits discharging or discriminating against an employee who reports a violation of commercial motor vehicle safety laws.

– Whistleblower Protection Act of 1989 upgrades the Office of Special Counsel, making it quasi-independent of the Merit Systems Protection Board.

At a conference on the legal protection of whistleblowers, every lawyer who spoke agreed that the laws do not work very well and that new laws rarely help. All were "whistleblower lawyers," most of whom had represented several whistleblowers. None pushed for new legislation. This is confirmed by my interviews with whistleblower lawyers.

None are particularly eager for new legislation. Nor are most whistle-blowers eager for new legislation, at least not of the type that Congress is remotely likely to pass. Legislation is the business of politicians, who may call a few whistleblowers to testify on behalf of their legislation.[6] After reviewing hundreds of laws protecting whistleblowers, Miethe (1999, 147–48) concludes that "there are statutory protections for whistleblowers in state and federal codes and protections in the common law under the public policy exceptions to the termination at-will doctrine. Unfortunately, most legal protection for whistleblowers is illusory; few whistleblowers are protected from retaliatory actions because of numerous loopholes and special conditions of these laws and the major disadvantage that individual plaintiffs have against corporate defendants."

Consider the case of Donald Rein, a senior environmental scientist, who brought a claim of reprisal under a Department of Energy (DOE) regulation in 1994 after he was terminated from his job after disclosing scientific flaws in an environmental study being conducted for the DOE by his employer. Rein won every stage of the process, from the initial investigative decision to the hearing officer's claim and the appeal before the deputy secretary, ultimately winning a judgment of $300,000 after four years of litigation.

Despite the agency's own decision on behalf of Rein, the DOE refused to require the contractor to pay the whistleblower, who has been out of work since his termination in 1994. Rein has declared bankruptcy and been unable to find work. Taking his case to U.S. District Court, Rein found a sympathetic judge who was unable to act. What follows is from U.S. District Court Judge Thomas Hogan's decision (Government Accountability Project press release, 7/1/98).[7]

> Because DOE has supported its promises with a mere Milquetoast of a regulation, essentially unenforceable in court, persons like [Rein] are left with little more than the promises of politicians and are held captive to the whim of an agency that may have far more tolerance of retaliation than it claims.... Thus, while plaintiff may perhaps seek to secure his judgment through another branch of government, the Court cannot prevent DOE from sitting idly as inspiring sound bytes echo aimlessly, giving little substance to hollow promises.

Unusual about this case is only that Rein found a federal judge to speak out on his behalf, even if the judge could not do much about it.

Time is on the side of the organization. Five years is not a long time for an organization to be involved in the courts; ten years is not unusual. But it is a long time for a whistleblower to be without a job, as the Rein case reveals. What one commentator says about the Defense Contractor Employee Protection from Reprisal Act of 1986 applies to many of the statutes. It "prescribes a path to an administrative determination through the bowels of DoD, creating a right without a remedy. Appeal apparently lies to the regional U.S. Court of Appeals" (Reynolds 1998, 66).

You work for Gigantic Defense Industries as an auditor. You complain about overcharging, first to your boss, then to the Department of Defense. You are fired, and the Department of Defense is expected to enforce your right to your job. This process may take several years and is unlikely to be resolved in your favor, given the historical reluctance of the Defense Department to overturn its contractors. You have a legal right to appeal to the U.S. Court of Appeals. This right will cost you at least $50,000 to exercise, which means just to get a judge to hear your case. The cost includes locating witnesses, deposing them, lawyers' fees, filing fees, and more. The case will drag on for years. Ten years is not unusual. Perhaps the court will decide in your favor, but probably not. Whistleblowers have won only four of almost ten thousand cases to reach the federal courts under the Whistleblower Protection Act of 1989.[8] One whistleblower I spoke with spent $100,000 just to get a federal judge to hear her case. "I had my day in court, only it wasn't a day, but a few minutes. The judge said I didn't have standing to sue, and I was back on the street $100,000 poorer."

How to understand the legal construction of the whistleblower? From a Foucauldian perspective, the real action is with nuts and sluts. The legal fiction of the protected whistleblower creates a person who may be exposed to the discipline that takes place within the framework of the law: mandatory psychiatric evaluations, investigations by private detectives, and the like. The purpose of the law is to expose the whistleblower to disciplinary power. The law works by constructing an individual who may be found to be a nut or a slut and thus not deserving of the law's protection.

The critique of liberal jurisprudence provides another perspective. It is the purpose of the law to enshrine existing power differences in society. It is not accidental but essential to the law that its procedures are on the side of the organization. That it takes five to ten years and a hundred thousand dollars to get one's day in federal court is not a neutral fact applicable to both parties. Like the law that forbids princes and paupers alike to sleep out under the bridge at night, legislation to protect whistleblowers must end up serving the organization against the unemployed and bankrupt middle-aged whistleblower, who worries if he will ever have enough money to retire. All this is, by the way, quite independent of the intent of the legislation, which is often benign. Not the intent of the legislation but the way in which the law serves those with the time and money to use it is the point.

All this is quite familiar, even if its basis in Foucault's critique of knowledge/power and the critique of liberal jurisprudence bestows on it a theoretical aura not every whistleblower would recognize. It is worth reflecting, however, on what the law looks like from the wrong end of the telescope, from the perspective of the whistleblower. From this perspective, the law is entirely capricious, government the province of men, not laws. "The law is a crap game, and the odds are against you. It all depends on who hears your case, and what he had for breakfast."

In part, the whistleblower is referring to the fact that cases are rarely clear-cut. Witnesses lie, and most judges hate to get involved in what they regard as personnel matters, an inclination that almost always favors the organization. The result is that *who* the judge or hearing examiner is makes all the difference in the world, a government of men not laws.

This is not what bothers the whistleblower most. What bothers the whistleblower most is that the legal issues involved are almost always procedural. To many theorists of democracy this is the point. To the whistleblower this is the problem. "Whether I win or lose has noting to do with what I did, whether I was right or wrong. No one cares about that. All they care about is that my boss followed the correct procedures in firing me."

And, the whistleblower might have added, whether he himself followed the correct procedures. Some states require that employees report violations first to their supervisors; otherwise they get no legal protection. Conversely, some federal workers (for instance, those at nuclear power plants) can be denied protection from wrongful discharge if they report their violation initially to their supervisor rather than to an external regulatory agency (Miethe 1999, 93–94). In the realm of whistleblower protection, procedure is king. Whistleblowers think this means that caprice rules. It is hard to say they are wrong.

One might argue that a procedural view of the law, however much it is disdained by whistleblowers, is at the heart of democratic theory. Certainly this is how most who write about the law see it, including Jürgen Habermas (1996) in his *Between Facts and Norms: Contributions to a Discourse Theory of Law and Democracy*. In fact, Habermas now finds in the procedures of Western law a mirror of what he calls the ideal speech situation, in which only the force of the better argument may prevail. That, in turn, is Habermas's famous definition of rationality.

It is a definition of rationality that when applied to the law has more in common with instrumental reason, not the perspective of the lifeworld which Habermas has defended for so many years. Who could argue, for example, that the rules of civil procedure have anything to do with ensuring the force of the better argument? The rules of civil procedure reflect a system imperative more concerned with preserving the predictability of outcomes than understanding (Chriss 1998).

Whistleblowers speak from the lifeworld. From this perspective, procedure and substance blend. Laws that protect whistleblowing while failing to protect the whistleblower make little sense. Justice means, says one whistleblower, that there is a "bridge to reality." In other words, justice means that someone outside the organization is willing to hear the whistleblower's story and possesses the power to make recompense, or at least to hear and understand, as Judge Thomas Hogan did. Even though the judge did nothing, Rein felt shriven. Someone outside the organization had heard and understood that the organization had acted with malice.

One might argue that it is an utterly naive view of justice, more the province of therapy. Perhaps it is, but we should consider what happens when justice becomes completely divorced from understanding:

when there is no longer any "bridge to reality" because procedure has become not a way of talking about substance but a substitute.

We should also consider what happens when justice becomes strictly the province of protected classes: that is, everyone but the ethically autonomous individual. One whistleblower put it this way: "I took advantage of laws against sex discrimination because they were available, and I'm glad I did. But I know they didn't fire me because I was a woman. Lots of women did fine [in the organization]. They fired me because I spoke out on a practice [of overbilling] that was near and dear to their hearts. But there aren't any laws to protect people who stand up and speak out when the company does something wrong. You have to belong to a special group to be protected."

In fact, there are laws to protect people in her situation. But her attorney advised her, correctly, that these laws are practically unenforceable, whereas the law on sexual discrimination contains provisions making it much easier to use. Mine is no argument against laws against sexual and racial discrimination. Mine is a political and theoretical point: that it is the autonomous ethical individual who is the real threat to the organization, and the law finds little room for such people. Or rather, it finds room for them as an idea in such a way as to render the individual behind the idea expendable.

One might argue that it is a purely practical matter, a question of fine-tuning the law. Few whistleblowers and their lawyers would agree, and it is from this group that one might expect the greatest push for legal reform. The law knows how to protect the individual from the state. The law has hardly a clue about how to protect the individual who resists the organization in the name of the public because our society has hardly a clue about what is public.

A POLITICAL ACTOR IN A NONPOLITICAL WORLD

Two stories about the de-politicized world of the whistleblower will help establish the relevance of my claim that the whistleblower is a political actor in a depoliticized world. The first is from the National Society of Professional Engineers' Board of Ethical Review (Case number 82–5, at www.niee.org/cases/). Engineer A is employed by a large defense contractor. He finds that one of the subcontractors is overcharging for substandard work. In other words, the subcontractor is defrauding the federal government. Management refuses to act, and Engineer A turns to his national society for evaluation and support. In its review, the national society quotes from its Code of Ethics Section II.1.a: "Engineers shall at all times recognize that their primary obligation is to protect the safety, health, property and welfare of the public. If their professional judgment is overruled under circumstances where the safety, health, property, or welfare of the public are endangered, they shall notify their employer or client or such other authority as may be appropriate." In other words, the code of ethics mandates whistleblowing.

In its review of the case, the national society found that Engineer A had legitimate cause for concern, concluding that "if an engineer feels strongly that an employer's course of conduct is improper when related to public concerns, and if the engineer feels compelled to blow the whistle to expose the facts as he sees them, he may well have to pay the price of loss of employment.... In this type of situation, we feel that the ethical duty or right of the engineer becomes a matter of personal conscience, but we are not willing to ... make the issue one for public discussion."

One finds the simple truth in surprising places. The National Society of Professional Engineers, whose members work for the largest corporations in the country, is not willing to make ethics a public matter. To be sure, in some circumstances, as when an organization is poisoning the water supply, it is another case. Overall, however, the society's position is to make ethics the realm of private sacrifice to a public world.

The second story concerns the legacy of a notorious medical malpractice case, in which the Dana-Farber Cancer Institute in Boston gave deadly overdoses of chemotherapy to several patients. In response, the state Board of Registration in Nursing has come up with new regulations, most of which have little to do with protecting patients (Gordon 1999).

> Because RNs have been fired for trying to protect their patients by exposing unsafe practices, nurses have begged state and federal officials

for whistle-blower legislation to protect them against employer retaliation. The Board of Registration in Nursing has not voiced support for
this effort.... What's more, the state board's proposed changes include
some ominous provisions. [One] would subject RN's to sanctions if
they engage in any conduct "which reflects or may reflect ... adversely
on the profession." Many nurse managers already regard informational
picketing, protest rallies, lobbying, and press criticism by their employees to be "unprofessional" and an embarrassment to their institutions.
This proposed rule would hand hospitals another club – in addition to
the threat of termination – to use against RN's who engage in patient
advocacy.

The engineers' professional association is, it seems, more public-
spirited than that of the nurses. While neither will become involved in
the politics of their professions, the engineers' association at least recognizes that public issues are involved, even if it will do nothing about
them. The nurses' association treats any attempt to politicize the issues as itself unprofessional. Professional, it seems, must mean private. Or rather, social, that strange and ubiquitous entity that seems to
have absorbed both private and public realms. according to Hannah
Arendt.

Much has been written about that important but puzzling entity that
Hannah Arendt calls "the social." One critic calls it "the blob" to suggest the vagueness of the concept. Let us be as simple and straightfor-
ward about it as possible. Used as a term of social and political criticism, the social is the absence of politics where politics belongs (Pitkin
1988, 252). This fits perfectly the professional associations, such as the
National Society of Professional Engineers. The professional associations might have made ethical conduct a public, that is, political matter. Overwhelmingly they have not (Glazer and Glazer 1989, 67–73).
The Nursing Board, already a public entity, might have decided to behave like one, rather than as an extension of the organization. To introduce politics into bureaucracy and society is not somehow to make
politics less pure or heroic. It is to make heroism possible.

The term "hero" meant originally one who participated in the Tro-
jan War and about whom a story could be told. To be a hero is to be
present and willing to act and speak in public and so begin a story of

one's own.[9] To be a hero means no more, and no less, than to be a citizen. To be a responsible citizen means not doubling. It means thinking like a public citizen (Ralph Nader's necessary redundancy) while working in the "proprietary" organization. To be a citizen in the organization is to be a sacrifice, for whom not even one's professional organization will speak.

One might argue that the subjects of discipline about whom Foucault writes, nuts and sluts, cannot be citizens because they lack the opportunity to become individuals in the first place and so become actors in their own stories. Certainly many whistleblowers seem to have trouble making sense of the stories they have begun, as well as trouble finding an ending.

But Foucault's perspective, like any theory, risks reifying its subjects, turning individuals into concepts, including the concept of subjects of discipline. It is the advantage of coming at theory from the perspective of the last man that these two terrible abstractions, society and disciplinary regimes, lose their reifying power – that is, their ability to turn individuals into concepts. When we look at the organization from the perspective of the last man, we can actually see the individual and what happens to him or her. Or rather, we see what remains of the subject after his sacrifice, the best evidence of his previous existence.

Social theory does not understand this very well. Either it writes about individuals as though they exist with rights and freedoms, able to express their opinions in various democratic fora. Or it writes in terms of the death of the individual, disciplined into nonexistence before he or she has a chance to be born into the world. Could it be that social theory goes to extremes because it cannot know an even more terrible truth–that individuals do exist, but the place where they spend most of their lives, the organization, is dedicated to their destruction?

Bauman is, I believe, one of the few social theorists who has confronted this reality, which is why this chapter begins with an epigraph from *Modernity and the Holocaust*, whose thesis is that every organization is dedicated to the destruction of its members' individuality, defined as the ability to think seriously about what one is doing. Arendt too knows that the organization is dedicated to the destruction of the individual. It is just that her account of society makes this truth more abstract than need be. In making it more abstract, she robs it of some of its insult.

Thoughtlessness

If the organization is the unit of analysis we should be concerned with, then we will have to rethink what the virtue of the organization man or woman consists of. For Max Weber, "the honor of the civil servant is vested in his ability to execute conscientiously the order of superior authorities, exactly as if the order agreed with his own conviction. This holds even if the order seems wrong to him and if, despite the civil servant's remonstrances, the authority insists on the order." This requires that the civil servant practice "moral discipline and self-denial in the highest sense" (Weber 1946, 95).

Putting it this way suggests an inner dialogue, an inner conflict between self and superior, insight and duty. Most whistleblowers are convinced that their colleagues do not participate in this inner dialogue. Instead, they describe their colleagues in terms that come closest to what Arendt calls thoughtlessness.

Thoughtlessness appears to stem from the experience of superfluity. Because everyone is replaceable, nothing anyone does really matters. Jane Bryan put it this way: "You know what [my co-worker] said? He said we might as well do it, because if we didn't the company would find someone else who would. So what difference did it make who did it. This way we'd at least keep our jobs." Soon it begins to sound as though no one is really doing anything.

Thoughtlessness is the medium of doubling, described in chapter 4 as a way of living in which one works terribly hard not to know what one is doing. The result is dissociation, a feeling that nothing is quite real. Or as Tom Delaney, the whistleblower with an imagination for consequences, put it, "The people around me acted like the were not releasing dangerous substances into the environment. They acted like they were not doing anything, like it was just pieces of paper, like they didn't represent anything real."

Thoughtlessness might more accurately be called fear of thought. People fear to think because they fear they may be fired, but this puts it a little too concretely. Bureaucracy teaches each member that he or she is "completely replaceable, and hence completely vulnerable to the whims of the institution" (Arendt 1973, 457–59). One bystander I spoke with who had observed unethical acts but had not blown the whistle said that he was afraid of losing his job and ending up on the street, like one of the homeless he stepped over every day on his way to work.

Instead of considering this fear to be strictly paranoid, we should recall the case of Peter J. Atherton, the nuclear engineer who may have lived in his car. It is the power to move the whistleblower so far to the margins that keeps the rest of us in line. Arendt calls these "exaggerated fears of ostracism and unemployment, of being unable to make a living and support their dependents" (Arendt 1978a, 231). From the perspective of the last man, these fears are not so exaggerated. We should consider whether the homeless do not perform an important social function in this regard, reminding us what the superfluous look like: just like you and me if we should happen to step outside the margins.

Particularly insidious is the way the organization transforms responsibility to family into a justification for anything. About the German bureaucrat, Arendt (1978a, 232–33) says, "It became clear that for the sake of his pension, his life insurance, the security of his wife and children, such a man was ready to sacrifice his beliefs, his honor, and his human dignity." All he asked in return was to be "fully exempted from responsibility."[10] In these circumstances, loyalty to family becomes loyalty to the boss. Or rather, they meld into one. To make responsibility to one's family the highest standard means that there is nothing one would not do for one's boss, who in effect becomes the father's father, or the mother's mother. The boss becomes head of the family.

It is an issue about which whistleblowers talk at length. They know that in blowing the whistle they have acted in the name of the entire family, just as rescuers of the Jews risked the lives of their families.[11] It may be moral and existential hubris to place one's family at risk, but there can be no morality without it. To be bound to others in love means to bind them to one's moral fate.

"Everyone has a family," said Jane Bryan. "Lots of my co-workers said, 'I'd go along with you, but I have a responsibility to my family.' But where does it stop? You could justify anything that way. I asked one if he would commit murder for his family, and he just looked at me as if I were crazy."

To succor oneself with the thought that one will do anything for one's family is tantamount to saying one will do anything: anything the boss says, to anyone he says to do it to. To think this way is to become completely irresponsible to the world. Here is how one who became this irresponsible put it, an engineer who was under pressure to fudge some test data.

> "You know ... I've been an engineer for a long time, and I've always believed that ethics and integrity were every bit as important as theorems and formulas, and never once has anything happened to change my beliefs. Now this. Hell, I've got two sons I've got to put through school and I just...." His voice trailed off. He sat for a few more minutes, then, looking over the top of his glasses, said hoarsely, "Well, it looks like we're licked. The way it stands now, we're to go ahead and prepare the data and other things for the graphic presentation in the report, and when we're finished, someone upstairs will actually write the report. After all ... we're just drawing some curves, and what happens to them after they leave here, well, we're not responsible for that." (Vandivier 1979, 168)

In just a few sentences the engineer has invoked just about every cliché of irresponsibility in the book. Does irresponsibility always speak in clichés? If so, they are clichés that bespeak a deeper fantasy – that the organization is nobody who is not really doing anything. Or at least it feels that way when one is working so hard not to be real.

While Arendt calls bureaucracy the rule of Nobody, it might be more accurate to call it the rule of the living dead, those who no longer exist as actors because they can no longer bear to think about what they are doing. More than a few whistleblowers talked about their bosses and co-workers as dead, or zombies. "Sometimes they just don't seem human," said one whistleblower of his co-workers. "I think people must kill a part of themselves to remain part of the system."

The result is loneliness, the most terrible loneliness of all, in which people no longer talk with themselves because they no longer know what they are doing. Or rather, because they no longer recognize that they are doing anything important. For most, loneliness is expressed in clinging to the crowd, doing anything not to become a space-walker. For a few, loneliness is expressed as a dreadful fear of alienation from their ego ideals, the best part of themselves.

Mary Manson, who blew the whistle on her company's accounting practices, put it this way: "I've never felt so forsaken in all my life as when I blew the whistle... no, that's not what I mean. I felt worse in the couple of years leading up to my blowing this whistle. Then I had to hide what I knew from myself as well as from [the other accountants]. Afterward at least I didn't have to hide from myself."

We should consider the possibility that whistleblowing is about trading off one dread for another. To remain within the system is to risk the dread of becoming dead to oneself. To step outside the system is to risk the dread of becoming dead to others. Martin Edwin Andersen put it this way:

> And those "friends" you've made, or thought you've made, at work over the years, during countless team projects, holiday parties, office birthdays, etc.? People you've laughed with, shared photos of your kids, and their latest love interest, and maybe even traveled with as part of your office's mission? The people about whom your spouse or significant other may have been jealous, because you spend more time with them during the day than you do with your loved one(s) nights and weekends. (And your nights and weekends end up being colored by what happened with "these people" during that long workweek.) Now, Whistleblower, you find you might as well have painted yourself green, stood on top of your desk, and shouted to your workmates that you're a closet Martian. Some will look away in embarrassment. Others will tell you to stop complaining and get back to "work." And still others will elbow your peers in a knowing sort of way and aver that they always knew that there was something just a tad touched about you.

For most it is the second choice that is most unbearable, to be the Martian, what Ellsberg calls the space-walker. (It is no accident that the same images of being cast adrift from the planet keep recurring. It is not just a matter of losing one's job but one's place in the world.) For a few it is the first choice that is worse, the risk of becoming dead to oneself. This does not make the whistleblower more authentic, whatever that means exactly. It just makes the whistleblower more fearful of a certain type of inauthenticity, perhaps more enraged about it as well: narcissistic rage at being expected to split or deaden oneself in order to fit in. That, as it turns out, may be enough to make a man or woman moral.

Thoughtlessness seems to be a way of not having to choose between loyalty to others and loyalty to oneself. In this regard, thoughtlessness is a lie, the pretense that one is living in a world in which it does not really matter what one does, for one is not really doing anything real. As another whistleblower put it, "I asked one of my friends at work why he didn't do anything. I thought he'd say he didn't want to lose his job. You know what he said? He said it didn't matter, that nothing we did made any difference anyway. He was talking about hundreds of kids who weren't getting services, and he said it didn't matter."

Thoughtlessness stems not merely, or even primarily, from fear. Thoughtlessness arises when we are unable to explain our fears – that is, make them meaningful, comprehensible, knowable. This happens when we lack the categories to bring our fears into being. Common narrative is, I've argued, of little help in this regard.

Social theory could be more helpful than it is. Liberal democratic theory assumes that politics is where the action is, and so it assumes that individualism is possible. Foucault's account assumes that individuals don't exist. Neither approach gets close enough to life in the organization, to say nothing of the lives of those who suffer the organization, to help individuals make sense of the forces arrayed against them.

One might argue that this is not the task of social theory, and perhaps it is not, but it is worth remembering that from time to time it has been. At its best, Marxism understood itself as a theory of the world capable of illuminating the situation of the least actor in terms that the least actor could understand, at least when the theory was interpreted for him by cadres. This practice was subject to terrible abuses, but that does not mean that the goal of a social theory that could make sense of the world to its subjects is not worthwhile. Nor must such a theory be merely descriptive, as Marxism reveals. It need only be material, which means that its abstractions should be constructed so that their instances are rendered more rather than less real. These instances are humans and their experiences, their lives. About how many social theories today can we say that they make their subjects more real?[12]

A PALINODE TO THE WHISTLEBLOWER

One way for the theorist to make his subjects more real is to fight with them, at least in his imagination. What is the worst thing I can think of to say about the whistleblower? Can I come up with a convincing reply? In fact, it is probably not so important that I convince myself, one way or the other, as that I engage in the dialectic.

The worst thing I can think of to say about the whistleblower is that he or she has become a whiner. What did you expect? If you wish to speak out against the practices of the organization, you must expect to pay the price. The strongest voice is that uttered on exit (Hirschman 1970). Resign with your eyes open, and do it with courage. Don't expect to disagree and be loved for your disagreement. Disagree, resign or be fired, go to the newspapers, and get on with your life.

Don't be like Johnny Dollar, the whistleblower who was fired from the Bureau of Engraving after going to a newspaper reporter over the bureau's lax security practices. Dollar spent the next six years of his life suing the bureau in federal court. He was not trying to get his job back. He'd reached retirement age and had not been denied his pension. Dollar sued to be officially recognized as a retired employee of the bureau so that he could remain a member of the Currency Club, where employees take their breaks and eat their lunch. There Dollar wanted to spend his days bad-mouthing the bureau and collecting the gossip that he published in his newsletter, which was dedicated to exposing scandals at the bureau.

It is not just whistleblowers who have difficulty resigning under protest. It is something that no one in American public life does well. In a postmortem on the Johnson administration, James Reston wrote that "the art of resigning on principle from positions close to the top of the American Government has almost disappeared. Nobody quits now" (Hirschman 1970, 118). A few still do, of course, or at least they act in such a way that they are prepared to be fired. In October 1969, six analysts of the RAND Corporation, under contract to the Defense Department to analyze the war in Vietnam, sent a letter to the *New York*

Times calling for the unilateral, speedy, and total withdrawal of United States forces. Although the protesters did not exit the organization, several said they consciously assumed the risk of "being exited." One of the six signers was Daniel Ellsberg (Hirschman 1970, 118).

This, as I said, is the strongest criticism I can level against whistle-blowers: you cannot be in and out at the same time, an antagonist and a valued employee. Choose one or the other and get on with it. If you protest policy, expect to "be exited," and get on with your life.

I thought this sometimes when listening to whistleblowers going on and on about their travails, though this does not mean I was right. It might just mean that I was tired of their pain. Since then I've thought long and hard about how valid this criticism is. In some cases it is valid. Johnny Dollar needs to grow up. But overall it is not a valid criticism, and Albert O. Hirschman's *Exit, Voice, and Loyalty* tells us why.

Hirschman assumes that exit will be noticed, and voice heard.[13] What happens when they are not? This is what the experience of superfluity means, the experience that discipline is aimed at creating: there is no point in objecting because you are not a person whose exit will be noticed or objection heard. Far from being a hero with a story, you are either placeholder or patient. Winston Smith's job was to rewrite history so that the one who ran afoul of the organization never existed in the first place. It sounds as though he did this to Bob Harris from chapter 2, who compares his situation to that of a tree falling in the forest when no one is there to hear.

It is the purpose of discipline to create a reality in which exit is unnoticed and voice unheard – not just by others but by the whistle-blower himself or herself. This is why the whistleblower cannot stop whining. He or she is not just whining. He or she is trying to figure out what in the world happened, an exploration that may sometimes sound like whining because it requires going over the same uncharted territory again and again. Only this is a little misleading. The term "territory" makes it sound like a place. The whistleblower has actually been cast into a place that is not place and a time that is not a time but endless and static at the same time, the topic of chapter 3.

From one perspective, a perspective that actually comes closest to the whistleblower's experience, discipline renders the whistleblower's act meaningless. Certainly this is how whistleblowers experience their stories. From another perspective, the task of discipline is not to render the whistleblower's act meaningless. It is to make the whistleblower him or herself available for sacrifice. The loss of political meaning achieved by discipline does not actually create a situation of meaninglessness. It creates a vacuum into which a more primitive meaning can flow, albeit unobserved, because this primitive meaning is so clothed in the rituals of rational discipline. This primitive meaning is the sacrifice of the scapegoat.

This thesis is the topic of the next chapter. It reveals Arendt's categories of thoughtlessness and superfluity to be accurate descriptions of the experience of organizational life, but not fundamental. Much the same may be said of Foucault's account of discipline. Thoughtlessness and superfluity defend against the dread of sacrifice, whereas discipline prepares the subject for it.

My thesis represents a perspective on whistleblowing more distant from the whistleblower's immediate experience but one in which the whistleblower would still recognize himself or herself. Certainly several whistleblowers who read this book in manuscript said they did. Many whistleblowers talk about themselves as scapegoats. What follows is a theoretical elaboration of this experience.

CHAPTER 7

The Political Theory of Sacrifice

You have seen how difficult it is to decipher the script with one's eyes; but our man deciphers it with his wounds. – Franz Kafka, *In the Penal Colony*

I T is far from wrong to state that the whistleblower is sacrificed as a lesson to others in the group, so that they will see the price of acting as an ethical individual who remembers that he or she belongs to the world. But this is not all that is going on with the sacrifice of the whistleblower. The whistleblower must know these truths for the rest of the organization, dying for the organization so that its members might live with these truths at a distance.

"When you blow the whistle, you become poison to the company," said one whistleblower. "Your presence makes them sick."

The Greek term for the scapegoat is *pharmakos*, which means both poison and cure. As pharmakos, the whistleblower is poison to the unity of the organization, which wants to obliterate every memory that the organization belongs to those outside its boundaries. In practice, this means obliterating individuals who remember the outside. Remembering is tantamount to thinking.

One sees an example of how powerful this poison is in the decision of the Internal Revenue Service (IRS) to fire Jennifer Long, the only one of seven agents who did not hide behind a curtain and did not wear a voice distortion mask (what the prisoners in Jeremy Bentham's Panopticon wore, so that they would not be shamed), while testifying before Congress about abuses at the agency. On Monday when she returned to work, said Long, every single manager was in her face with the same refrain: "You're not a team player."

The chairman of the Senate Finance Committee, William Roth, had warned the IRS not to retaliate against Long, and a year later he warned the commissioner in follow-up hearings. Two days later, on April 15, the Houston office of the IRS, where Long worked, fired her, after spending a year documenting thirty-three alleged shortcomings, including the failure to write neatly in her appointment book.

Senator Roth went ballistic, the new commissioner of the IRS saw red, and the story made the front page of the *New York Times*, which wrote about the "pathology of an ingrained culture" at the district office. Long will not be fired, and her supervisors will be punished, the reader is relieved to learn, but consider that her supervisors must have known that they were risking their jobs to take hers. In effect, they were committing career suicide. They just couldn't stand it. They or she had to go, and this is one of the rare cases in which it was they, at least for now (Johnston 1999).

If the pharmakos is poison, he or she is also the cure, though not in the ethical sense. Rarely do the actions of the scapegoat stimulate others to stand up and be counted. The pharmakos is cure in the sense that the original scapegoat is cure. He represents what we all have learned about the organization but cannot bear to know: that it will destroy us if we think about what we are doing and what is happening to us. So we hold our knowledge at a distance, in the mind and body of the scapegoat. That is, after all, the purpose of the scapegoat: not just to dispose of our sins but to let us know them at a safe distance, so we might contemplate them as though they belonged to someone else.

It is a cruel distance, requiring not just the isolation of the whistleblower but his isolation in the face of the togetherness of his tormentors. To be a whistleblower is to be without colleagues and friends. "I learned the meaning of loneliness and alienation," said one whistleblower, the former medical director of a drug company, about his life in the months after he blew the whistle (Glazer and Glazer 1989, 43).

The original scapegoat, we recall, is not killed but driven into the featureless desert. As though to say this is the cost of being an individual in the organization. This is the same language used by Molly Higgins, referring to how she and her husband were transferred to a series of ever more remote military bases. "They kill you, they isolate you in the desert."

The most important thing about the scapegoat is that he or she is arbitrary, like the original Hebrew scapegoat, chosen by lot. René Girard (1977, 236–37, 311–12) says this in his study of the scapegoat. It is not strictly true, of course. The Jew was not an arbitrary scapegoat but a historically practiced one. Nor is the whistleblower arbitrary. If the whistleblower did not speak out, he or she would not be sacrificed. But as soon as he or she does so, it matters little who the whistleblower is. Not only are age and rank in the organization no protection, but they frequently make the whistleblower more vulnerable to reprisal, as several studies of professional whistleblowers reveal (Devine 1998).

One might argue that I have missed the point. The whistleblower has already identified him or herself by speaking out, and what we must figure out is "who" is speaking. I have suggested that doing so is itself likely to become an instance of social scientific discipline, at least as it is usually practiced, as the study of whistleblower psychology. Once the whistleblower speaks out, his or her experiences are remarkably similar to those of other whistleblowers. Let us try to learn from this, lest we plumb the depths of whistleblower psychology only to escape the terrible surface of his or her experience.

CONTAINING INDIVIDUALITY

Girard (1977, 18, 36) argues that ritual sacrifice arose and is maintained by the need of the organization, be it tribe or nation, to contain the violence within, violence that threatens to engulf the organization in bloody, Hobbesian conflict: the war of all against all. The violence that the organization directs against outsiders and internal miscreants always threatens to overflow its bounds and engulf the entire society. The scapegoat is sacrificed in the hope that the cycle of impure violence could be contained by an act of purifying, controlled violence: "The sacrificial process furnishes an outlet for those violent impulses that cannot be mastered by self-restraint.... All concepts of impurity stem ultimately from the community's fear of a perpetual cycle of violence arising in its midst.... The function of [sacrificial] ritual is to 'purify' violence; that is, to 'trick' violence into spending itself on victims whose death will provoke no reprisals." Girard is writing about the origins of sacrifice. What sacrifice looks like now, he says, is law.

In defining the organization, I argued that it is mistaken to think of whistleblowing as an issue of group loyalty versus individual transgression by the whistleblower. Instead, it is an issue of organizational transgression versus individual transgression. Transgression is, in other words, the way of the world. The organization is an instrument of transgression.

Civilization is transgression, and organized transgression is the mark of developed civilization. The problem is that organized transgression always threatens to get out of hand. It threatens to turn in on itself, to transgress itself, as Jennifer Long's supervisors did. It is for this reason that the organization turns to the scapegoat. In destroying the scapegoat, the organization reenacts in miniature the self-transgression that would destroy it and so contains and limits these destructive forces by giving them symbolic outlet.

So far, my analysis of transgression mirrors Girard's. What he calls violence I call transgression, a term that includes violence as well as all the other ways organizations trespass on others, from lawsuits to monopoly prices. From here on I diverge from Girard, believing that he has it not just wrong but backward, always a more interesting mistake. In spite of his profound insight into the importance of sacrifice in social life, Girard has made the mistake of most sociologists. That mistake is the mistake of Hobbes: presuming that the problem is the anomic, presocial individual, always waiting for the breakdown of law and order so that he or she can run amok. Sacrifice ritualizes this anomic tendency and so organizes it as a collective act against the one. In so doing it protects order.

What if this has it backward? Sacrifice serves not to contain and channel the ever-present threat of individual violence but the ever-present threat of individual morality. It is against this disruptive moral behavior that sacrifice is mobilized. Sacrifice serves not to rechannel destructive violence. Sacrifice serves to rechannel destructive individual morality that might result in the breakdown of organizational control and hierarchy. Sacrifice is mobilized against thought in the name of organizational autarky.

One might argue that Girard was right then but not now. In the premodern era, before the rise of large-scale social organization, the leading threat was the outbreak of Hobbesian violence, the war of all against all. Today, the threat is the violence of the large organization itself. The Holocaust epitomizes this threat, which has made this century the bloodiest in world history.

The trouble with this argument is that there was lots of large-scale social organization in the premodern era, including dynastic China and the Roman Empire. Furthermore, outbreaks of violence about which Girard writes, the war of all against all, are rare. It is almost always group conflict that threatens the social order, what the Greeks called *stasis*, intense factional conflict, like the civil war in Corcyra about which Thucydides (*History*, 3.69–85) wrote.

In conditions of stasis, the real problem is who is in and who is out and where to draw the boundaries. It is in this situation, the situation of most organizations most of the time, that outbreaks of individual morality are so dangerous. For it is the mark of individual morality that it speaks from a position at once inside and outside the organization.

In this circumstance, one who speaks from the outside is what Sartre calls *visqueux*, a viscous boundary crosser, outside and inside at the same time. The anthropologist Mary Douglas (1966) uses the term "slimy" to capture the fear of one who will not stay in his place, or rather, one whose place we do not even know. It is what every organization is most afraid of: that someone inside represents the interests of outside, that the organization cannot control its own boundaries, that it does not even know them. It is what Jennifer Long's supervisors meant when they accused her of not being a team player. The language is banal, but the sentiment is profound, reflecting the deepest fears of organizational man and woman.

This accounts, I believe, for that otherwise puzzling empirical finding. Internal whistleblowers are about as likely to be punished as external whistleblowers. If you go to your boss with the problem, you are almost as likely to be fired as if you go directly to the newspapers (Miethe 1999, 80; Rothschild and Miethe 1996, 15–16). The whistleblower does not necessarily need to go public to get into trouble because once he mentions his or her concerns he or she already is the public inside the organization. It is the only unforgivable organizational sin, to become the outside on the inside.

Recall the executive who said that what is right in the corporation is not what is right in a man's home or church. What's right in the corporation is what the guy above wants from you. The whistleblower is so threatening because he or she brings the values of the home and church – the larger world – into the organization.

The whistleblower, it is apparent, need not speak out in the name of the public within the organization in order to get into trouble. He or she need only speak as though he or she were a member of the public, as if he or she remembered his or her membership in the world. An imagination for consequences, a sense of the historical moment, identification with the victim, a reluctance to double, a sense of shame: each is a dagger pointed at the heart of the organization. To think and act in terms of these stories is to be a political actor in a nonpolitical space. Not because this space, on margin of the organization, is not properly political, but because our laws cannot make any sense of this space because our political tradition cannot.

In this space the whistleblower is granted legal protection in a way that reveals all the ironies of liberalism, captured by the story about the prince, the pauper, and the bridge. To act politically in this depoliticized public space is to be a scapegoat. In this regard, at least, the law is true to its original purpose according to Girard, sacrificing the individual so the group can be safe.

The purpose of sacrificing the whistleblower is to prevent the outbreak of an epidemic of ethical and moral responsibility that would threaten to engulf the organization, destroying its ability (or so its members fear) to maintain its boundless autonomy in a hostile world. Sacrifice always aims at halting an epidemic, in this case of individuality, as though it could be spread by example. Perhaps it can. Its spread is halted by making the boundary between inside and outside as clear as possible. The real threat posed by the whistleblower is to remind the organization that it belongs to the larger world. This is what thought represents – a way of thinking whose boundaries are not those of the organization.

To deter this way of thinking, the whistleblower must be moved to the margins: not just of the organization but of society. The task is complete not when the whistleblower is dismissed but when he is blacklisted from any "sister companies." The task is complete when a fifty-five-year-old engineer delivers pizza to pay the rent on a two-room walkup.

THE TRAFFIC BETWEEN MARGIN AND CENTER
IS A TWO-WAY STREET

The movement of the whistleblower to the margins is only half the story. The other half is the way in which the destruction of the whistleblower represents the movement of power that is usually present only from the margins to the center. As the whistleblower is moved to the margin, the power that moves him there makes a brief appearance at the center of society, reminding us of its existence.

Civilization, says Norbert Elias (1994, 450), is a process of shifting powerful and disturbing emotions and experiences, such as sadism and violence, from the center to the borderlines of society. There they are not lessened or mitigated but contained and stored up behind the scenes, in military barracks, police stations, and prisons, ready to be called upon in times of unrest and exerting a continuous threat to those who would challenge the regime. "A continuous, uniform pressure is exerted on individual life by the physical violence stored behind the scenes of everyday life, a pressure totally familiar and hardly perceived."

Not the opposite of Foucault's argument, the account of Elias differs at decisive points. Both recognize, for example, that elimination of public torture does not mean that the power behind it has disappeared or become merely rational. Whereas Foucault sees the power as changing its form, becoming tantamount to knowledge, Elias sees only that power changes its locus, becoming more compact and focused, so to speak. From Elias's perspective, Foucault came upon this process in midstream, confusing the borderline location of these reservoirs of power with the origins of a new type of power, tantamount to knowledge. The location may be new, but the power is not.

Margin to center, or center to margin, each assumes that center and margins are places from which one moves, one way or the other. What if they are not? What if center and margin are the axes along which power constantly travels? If this is so, then it is misleading to ask where is power located. The key question is how power *moves*. I am arguing that power moves not just in those small structuring spaces that create individuals and practices (though the microphysics of power is important) but between the margins and the center and back again. In other words, we make dichotomies – center or margin – out of what should really be axes. Power is always on the move, and one of its well-trod paths is between margin and center. In opposing the older image of the sovereign head, Foucault would put the hydra head, many loci of power. In fact, both these images are static. Not creatures with power but the movement of power itself is what we should think about. Sometimes Foucault writes about power in this way, sometimes not.

An example from Elias (1994, 99) will help put flesh on the bones of this abstraction. Once, says Elias, the carving of meat was a spectacle, the host celebrating his guests by carving the whole animal at the table. Gradually, however, the spectacle is felt to be distasteful, an insult to civilized sensibilities. Carving does not disappear, however. People still eat meat. Rather, the distasteful is removed behind the scenes of social life. Specialists take care of it in the butcher shop or kitchen.

> It will be seen again and again how characteristic of the whole process of civilization is this movement of segregation, this hiding "behind the scenes" of what has become distasteful. The curve running from the carving of a large part of the animal or even the whole animal at table, through the advance in the threshold of repugnance at the sight of dead animals, to the removal of carving to specialized enclaves behind the scenes, is a typical civilization curve.

Here it is good to recall that the carving of the animal at the table was not just a hospitable act. It is the paradigm of all sacrifice, a sacrificial drama replayed every time we carve a turkey or roast for our family and friends. The body of the pharmakos, the sacrifice, is first offered to the gods. But it is eaten by man.

Prisons, asylums, and other total institutions about which Foucault writes represent not power that originates at the margins but power that has been moved to the margins from the center, while losing none of its centrality. The civilization curve that moves the hanging from the town square to the prison basement is not so much a refinement of power as it is a veiling of it.

For Foucault (1979) it is the Panopticon, Jeremy Bentham's prison in which inmates are always visible to the gaze, that epitomizes disciplinary power. We should consider that the real paradigm of modern power is the veil. But a strange veil it is, intensifying the reality of what it conceals, the martial power of the state. But then veils have always done that, panopticons of the imagination. Whistleblowers lift the veil for a moment. Instead of looking at what lies behind the veil, we gaze at the one who lifts it. In this way we perpetuate the problem that Foucault identifies, transforming whistleblowing into deviance. This is true even if we admire the deviant.

While prisons, asylums, and other total institutions represent the power that has been moved to the margins, these institutions have their correlates at the center: all the other organizations of society, such as corporations, government agencies, private associations, small businesses, schools, and colleges. That is, the place where whistleblowers, and most of the rest of us, work. Rather than calling these organizations correlates, it might be more accurate to call them mirror images. The power that lords it over the surface in the total institution hides just under the surface in the institutions closer to the center of society. But not too far under the surface, lest we fail to remember its presence.

The sacrifice of the whistleblower has more the quality of the torture of Winston Smith than it does the public torture of Robert-François Damiens, with which Foucault (1979) famously begins *Discipline and Punish*. The sacrifice of the whistleblower is neither discipline nor an act of public political power upon his body, but something in-between. Or maybe it is just something different, a public demonstration that takes place in private. It is this that makes it so hard for the whistleblower to frame and form his or her narrative. It is almost as though it didn't happen.

"Sometimes it's as if nothing happened," said Wanda Freed. "Like they didn't really do anything to me, like one day I just left. I know it's not true, I know they fired me because I [reported the agency director], but they made it seem like it wasn't about that, like I just didn't fit in or something. Sometimes I wonder if I ever really worked there."

If the whistleblower's sacrifice is private and hidden, this does not mean that he or she is subject to a new form of power. It only means that power is moving around in ways social theory does not quite comprehend.

A surprising number of whistleblowers, about 30 percent of those I have listened to, have been removed from their offices, or not allowed to enter them, by men with guns: private or government security guards. The whistleblower does not forget the experience, frequently describing the gun in some detail. In no case have the men with guns been called as a last resort, because the whistleblower refused to leave. The guns were a first resort. No whistleblower I have spoken with has been removed at gunpoint, but that hardly matters. The gun is there, carried by the man who escorts the whistleblower to the door or prevents him from entering. That, or the gun is just a phone call away. In the last analysis civilization rests on men with guns.

To be sure, the whistleblowers I spoke with were overrepresented in government agencies with security concerns, such as the Department of Energy, Nuclear Regulatory Commission, Bureau of Engraving, and Department of State. But some whistleblowers in private organizations have reported similar experiences. Degradation ceremonies they might be called: the whistleblower is summoned to his boss's office, fired, taken to his old office in the presence of armed guards who allow him to fill a cardboard box with mementos such as family photos, but no papers, computers, or disks. Finally, he is escorted to the front door carrying his little box as though it were his coffin.

These are not just degradation ceremonies. They are a form of public execution, designed to remind those who remain of the power of the organization to reach anywhere in a moment. All this does not make Foucault simply mistaken about capillary power, as he calls it: power that migrates from the periphery to the center, his model of disciplinary power. It means that capillaries carry blood and power in both directions, so that we see at the margins more clearly the brutality, tyranny, and charisma of everyday life, displaced there – sovereigns not in exile but in waiting.

What is so striking about this power is the way that it can move the margin to the center in a moment, which is precisely what happens with the whistleblower: power moves from the margin to the center, moving back to the margin and carrying the whistleblower with it. Moved to the margins and rendered more invisible, power has not therefore become more subtle. Power has just gone underground, which means that it is able to emerge anywhere in an instant, but generally does not have to, precisely because we know it's there. From time to time the whistleblower reminds us.

"Nietzsche is the philosopher... who managed to think of power without having to confine himself within a political theory to do so," says Foucault (1980b, 53). It would be easy to say that Foucault has confused Nietzsche's metaphysics of structureless power (or rather, the metaphysics of power that is its own structure) with a politics of power without political structures. Only that would put it too sharply. Instead, Foucault has written about disciplinary power in a way that makes it more difficult than need be to see its connection to the structures of political power. An advantage of looking at whistleblowers, men and women who have been thrust to the margins by what sometimes looks like disciplinary power but is actually much closer to arche, is that it highlights the connection between powers.

Institutionalized violence and coercion are everywhere in ordinary public life, even if they are not generally recognized. What is remarkable about the organization, that entity in which the whistleblower works, is the way it draws on public power not just for private ends (a fact that has been known for centuries) but the way it uses public coercion to create a space in which it may enact an essentially public ritual, sacrifice, for a strictly private end, organizational autarky.

The whistleblower generally does not see this, at least not for some time. He or she is too close. The result is not just that the whistleblower is overly reliant on the law he loves to hate but that he has trouble figuring out what happened to him and so cannot tell a story about it. As he tells it, the story is idiosyncratic, and yet it is a tale as old as the individual and the state. It is older even, as old as Leviticus.

What I have not been able to describe very well is the way in which many whistleblowers come to learn these truths. If they did not, I would not know them, for almost everything I have learned about whistleblowing I have learned from them. It takes the whistleblower a while to figure it out, generally at least a decade, often longer. Some never do. I would like to be able to say that when they do figure it out, they are in some sense liberated, at least insofar as they can take up the position of the dead. Only it is not true.

Knowledge and what one is able to do with it are two different things. Not entirely different, of course, but different enough so that there is no guarantee that understanding brings even the compensation of truth. For many whistleblowers the truth is not good enough and never will be. But even here we learn something. The whistleblower destroyed is still an individual. That individuals can be destroyed does not demonstrate that the individual does not exist. Who would say this about Winston Smith or Julia? On the contrary, the existence of broken men and women proves the existence of man and woman.

THE SACRED AND DREADFUL ORGANIZATION

In *The Altruistic Personality*, Oliner and Oliner (1988, 2) conclude that most did not rescue because they did not care enough. "Clearly, then, even many basically good and decent folk ... nonetheless regarded the fate of others as separate and distinct from their own – not quite pertinent enough, not quite important enough to compel intervention."

I have suggested a different explanation. Carelessness is not the reason most don't speak out. Dread is the reason most don't speak out, even though this dread may sometimes look like carelessness – what Arendt calls thoughtlessness. Thoughtlessness does not come naturally. We have to work hard to be thoughtless, but fear is a good motivator, the fear of becoming the sacrifice, the space-walker.

Wounded narcissism is, I have hypothesized, one of the few experiences powerful enough to overcome the dread of being sacrificed. Or rather, wounded narcissism, the fear that one's self is about to lose all value because it is about to lose its already tenuous connection to its ego ideal, is an even more dreadful dread. What I called choiceless choice is actually about choosing the dread you will live for against the one you fear to die for.

To defy the organization is to subject oneself to the discipline about which Foucault writes. Still, it would be mistaken to think that ours has become a world of rational discipline. Ours is a world in which discipline serves sacred purposes whose sacredness has long been forgotten. When we forget what we are doing, upholding a transcendent order, it does not mean that we are no longer doing it. It only means that we no longer know what we are doing. The sacrifice of the whistleblower could remind us, if we would let it.

If we remembered what we were doing, we might be less likely to treat particular organizations as though they were sacred. We might, in other words, be able to distinguish between particular organizations and the transcendent power of society. Expressed in terms of ideas attached to authors, we might be a little less likely to think about the sacred as Shils does and a little more like Durkheim.

For Shils (1982, part 2), the sacred attaches not to the moral foundations of society but to the power centers of society and their symbols, from crowns and limousines to men with guns. This is why, Shils argues, an order from a superior is experienced (even if we no longer know it) not simply as a rational command but as an utterance that shares in a transcendent moral order, the point of the long quotation from Shils in chapter 1. Disobedience becomes tantamount to sacrilege, though hardly anyone ever puts it that way. Whistleblowers don't put it this way either; they just feel in their bones what it is to be impure.

It might be helpful to think about the sacred more the way Shils's predecessor Emile Durkheim (1933, 1965) did. For Durkheim, it is not the power centers of society but society itself (what he calls the "conscience collective" in an early work) that is sacred.[1] Not because society participates in a transcendent order, but because of the way individuals depend on society for the meaning and existence of their lives. It is in the awe-inspiring gap between individual and society that Durkheim locates the sacred. The more we prattle on about individualism, the less we shall know it. Not because it isn't true, and not because individuals don't exist (I have spent much of this book arguing that they do), but because we have become alienated from this dimension of the sacred that makes the individual worthwhile, his or her participation in this larger order.

Not even academics have much use for this aspect of Durkheim's thought these days. And surely it is true that there is not much left of the sacred in our modern, rationalized world, even as Durkheim claimed to see its residue in such basic values as "thou shalt not murder." If, however, we were to see the sacred in the basic values of society, not just its power centers, then it might be easier to see that challenging the organization may itself be a sacred act.

Sacred is not just power but the conscience collective, the values that make this society a meaningful one to live in. It is these same values that the organization is organized to deny in the service of instrumental reason, as Bauman argues. To be a whistleblower is to assert the conscience collective in the midst of the organization. To be a whistleblower is to set one way of thinking about the sacred, the conscience collective, against another, sacred power. Only when we know this will we truly understand what is going on with the whistleblower.

In this superficially rationalized world, in which all the bits and bytes and flashing lights have blinded us to the power of the sacred in the midst of the social, it is more important than ever before to know this. The sacrifice of the whistleblower is a sacred ritual, clothed in the rituals of rationality. But if the whistleblower's sacrifice is sacred, so too is the whistleblower, blessed and cursed with a terrible knowledge. I have tried to listen to the whistleblower with the seriousness this knowledge deserves.

Appendix on Problems of Confidentiality

MORE than in any other book I have written, I have disguised identities. Not only are all names pseudonyms (unless otherwise noted), but I have changed the names of the organizations where many whistleblowers worked.

While many of my subjects signed an informed consent document on file with the Human Subjects Review Committee of my academic department, not all did so. The document promises confidentiality.

Some whistleblowers desperately want their stories told, and a few were unwilling to sign because they insisted I use their names.

Some interviews were over the telephone. The whistleblower saw my name in the newspaper, or on a whistleblower web site, and called or wrote me. Sometimes the conversations were brief, sometimes they went on for hours. In either case, there was no opportunity for the whistleblower to sign a consent form. I did, however, publish my consent form on the web site where I advertised my interest in whistleblowing, so that some who called or wrote had an opportunity to see it.

Some whistleblowers are scared and would not sign anything under any circumstances. On one or two occasions, whistleblowers apparently used pseudonyms without informing me.

Most of the whistleblowers I spoke with have little chance of getting their jobs back. Many do not want them. Some, however, are still in court, others hope to get their jobs back, and still others do not want to be put on an informal blacklist. A few are still working where they blew the whistle.

One is an undercover informant for a law enforcement agency, a fact I wish I did not know. In a couple of cases, protecting the whistleblower's identity might mean protecting the possibility that the whistleblower could continue or resume his or her career. I cannot imagine that it would affect whether the whistleblower received a legal settlement.

The number of whistleblowers who have publicized their own cases far exceeds the number who want (or, in my opinion, need) confidentiality. Nevertheless, the only good policy is consistency, and I have disguised all identities. The only exceptions are Peter J. Atherton, Daniel Ellsberg, the late Ron Ridenhour, and Lawrence Rockwood, whose cases are so widely known that disguise would be pointless. I have also used the real names of a couple of whistleblowers who asked that I do so if I should quote from their letters or e-mails to me. Of course, I have also used the real names of whistleblowers whose cases I read about in newspapers and magazines but with whom I have not spoken. In quoting whistleblowers whose stories were published in books and journals, I quoted the name as it appears in the source, which was sometimes real, sometimes not.

Much of my time was spent listening to whistleblowers talk among themselves in groups. I do not believe there was ever a time where every member of the group did not know that I was a researcher, not a whistleblower. I told every member, and every new member, and distributed my statement of confidentiality and informed consent to every member of the group, even if not every group member signed and returned it.

I am not the only whistleblower researcher to face these problems. Elliston et al. (1985b, 77–84) state that the more they thought and talked about it, the more they realized how difficult the issue was. Even assuming everyone whose name was released had signed a consent form, releasing their names might implicate others. Even the much reviled boss, to whom I have repeatedly referred, deserves the protection of anonymity, especially since he or she has not told his or her side of the story.

Using a pseudonym but referring to the real role and the organization might not solve this problem because many whistleblower cases are quite well known. The most dramatic solution to this problem, say Elliston et al., "would require all names to be deleted – the names of individuals, organizations, the state, and titles of offices. It was to this solution that we were eventually driven.... Only such a drastic measure would be certain to protect the identities of those who had spoken to us in confidence" (84).

But the situation is even more problematic than this. Many whistleblower cases are so well known, at least by those within the organization, that pseudonyms do not suffice. How many people blew the whistle on the NRC almost twenty years ago, only to have their predictions come true in the last few years? How many released the Pentagon Papers? How many were court-martialed for conducting their own inspections of a Haitian prison? Elliston et al. (1985b, 91) put it this way.

"Those who are familiar with scandals and exposés could recognize a famous incident from the story that was told. To change the names without changing the incriminating evidence would stop short of all that could be done to protect the identity of our informants. Accordingly, we found it necessary, in the name of confidentiality, to tell a story, to invent a new story."

This, though, is a slippery slope. Once one has changed the names, both individual and organizational, the roles, and the facts, then the stories one tells come awfully close to fiction. Elliston et al. accept this, quoting Sartre to the effect that "I have the feeling of doing a work of pure imagination" (91). I do not accept that, but that does not mean I have a neat solution.

The policy I have followed is that if I obtained the whistleblower's informed consent (which includes a promise of anonymity), worked closely with the individual whistleblower, and shared a draft version of this book manuscript with the whistleblower (as I did with almost a dozen), then I changed relatively little. I might, however, have changed the sex of the whistleblower. This was relatively easy to do because there was little difference between male and female whistleblowers other than their sex.

The more these three standards were not fulfilled, the more details I altered. I occasionally attributed quotations from one source to two different people working at two different but similar organizations. Once or twice I attributed quotations from two different people in similar organizations to one source. All quotes are verbatim.

In general, the principle of disguise I followed was parallelism. Try to tell the same story, but set it in a different organization. The Department of Energy might become the Environmental Protection Agency, if that made sense. If I attributed one long quotation to two different people, I made sure that both worked in similar organizations in similar positions.

My solution is not elegant, and I am not especially pleased with it. Most important, however, is to protect the whistleblower. Second most important is to share my practices with the reader.

Notes

ONE: INTRODUCTION

1. In *Not Saussure: A Critique of Post-Saussurean Literary Theory*, Raymond Tallis (1995) argues that much postmodernism stems from a disappointment with this impossible ideal: that thought and action, insight and achievement, will and capability, the actual and the ideal, and above all the particular and the general, may someday in some theory (or in some utopian practice?) become one. If this cannot be, then Jacques Lacan and Jacques Derrida will have none of it. All generalities will be a lie, all particulars contingent on the reigning fiction. Theodor Adorno (1974) shared in this ideal but responded to its absence with a more delicate spirit of disappointment. I have tried to follow his example.

2. The stereotype of Socrates is of a man who goes around asking *other* people how they define terms like "justice." True enough, but he also spends a lot of time talking to himself about what he should do, even as one of the partners in this dialogue sometimes has the quality of another self; Socrates' daimon is "a sort of voice which comes to me, and when it comes it always dissuades me from what I am proposing to do" (*Apology* 31d).

3. Individualism is the doctrine of individuality, and individualism is complex. Among other things, individualism is an account of the dignity of humanity, with roots reaching back to the Hebrew Bible. Individualism is an epistemological doctrine of the origin of knowledge in individual perception. Individualism is a metaphysical assumption that it is the separate individual who is most real, and it is an ethical doctrine that morality rests on individual decision. Individualism is also an economic and political ideal. See Stephen Lukes's (1973) *Individualism* for something of the richness of the concept.

4. There has been some research on "the whistleblowing personality," as it is sometimes called (Jos, Tompkins, and Hays 1989; Miceli and Near 1992; Miethe 1999, 50–54). Overall, however, the psychology of whistleblowers is

less developed territory than that of rescuers, a situation that has its advantages. Those who write about whistleblowers are less likely to invoke it as an explanation than those who write about rescuers. More research on whistleblowers may change this situation, which will not necessarily be progress.

5. Even if rescuers score high on religiosity, for example, tens of millions of nonrescuers would score equally high or higher. By confining their sample of nonrescuers to a population roughly one-quarter the size of the sample of rescuers (when they might have made it a hundred times larger; there is no shortage of nonrescuers to interview), Oliner and Oliner downplay this compelling fact: tens, and perhaps hundreds of millions of men and women who would score as high or higher on religiosity as rescuers did nothing. The same can be said of every one of their categories.

6. Age, class, family background, religious belief, friendship with Jews, and involvement in community activity are the categories drawn upon by Oliner and Oliner, all the usual social psychological suspects, and none is sufficiently subtle and sensitive to make the distinction between rescuer and bystander. What Oliner and Oliner (1988, 312, Table 7.15) do, of course, is add all the differences up and together call these differences "extensivity." It is not the best way to do social science.

7. Aware of this problem, Tec (1986) says that although standard social psychological categories do not distinguish rescuers from nonrescuers, there are more subtle correlates, or "cluster of shared characteristics," as she calls them, not reducible to social class, religion, parental values, or education. Prime among these is social marginality. The difficulty with this solution is that social marginality is anything that either the rescuer, the rescued, or Tec finds unusual, such as the fact that a rescuer was not friendly with his neighbors. Tec (1986, 189) has no basis to say that rescuers were more marginal than nonrescuers, only that in retrospect rescuers were "on the periphery of their community" in some way, which includes having different ideas. In effect, Tec ends up defining marginality as helping Jews. It is true, of course, but it is no explanation, just a description. Compare Tec's account with Kristen Monroe's *The Heart of Altruism* (1996), which demonstrates that it is possible to carefully describe the worldview of the rescuer without pretending one is explaining the origin of rescuer behavior. In Monroe's case, less is more.

TWO: DON'T JUST DO IT TO SAVE LIVES

1. Miethe (1999, 58) includes among whistleblowers those who blow the whistle on misconduct directed solely against themselves.

2. The statistical characteristics of the whistleblowers I worked with match almost perfectly the characteristics of whistleblowers in Miethe's (1999) *Whistleblowing at Work*, the most extensive study yet, based on interviews with hundreds of whistleblowers. Miethe also interviewed hundreds who saw abuse but did not blow the whistle, a valuable comparison I occasionally draw on.

3. One reason the number fired for internal whistleblowing is so high is that if you just go to your boss you generally don't acquire privileged status under most laws protecting whistleblowers. For that you have to go outside the organization. If you just go to the boss, it's easier to fire you. Elliston et al. (1985b, 1–15) would restrict whistleblowing to the act of going public. It is not whistleblowing, but something else, more like politics and persuasion within the organization, to go to one's boss's boss. Though this restriction might make sense if the issue were primarily one of clear definition, it would exclude from view that most fascinating observation: there is not much difference between going public and going to the boss's boss as far as retaliation is concerned. In either case one has identified oneself as someone whose loyalties lie elsewhere, and that is enough. Definitions should serve theory, or at least the interesting observation. For this reason I reject Elliston's distinction, even though his *Whistleblowing Research* contains a remarkably intelligent discussion of problems of definition (1985b, 1–17).

   In "Whistleblowing: A Restrictive Definition and Interpretation," Peter Jubb (1999) defines whistleblowing even more narrowly, almost equating it with civil disobedience. Though his definition has the advantage of emphasizing that whistleblowing is a political act, it could obscure the fact that organizations often succeed in turning dissent into an occasion for discipline. That is, the organization prevents whistleblowing from becoming a public act in the first place. This is the topic of chapters 6 and 7.

4. Bauman's book is titled *Modernity and the Holocaust*, but he is writing about every modern organization, not just the ones that made the Holocaust. Indeed, that is the thesis of his book.

5. I don't know how I could prove this statement within the compass of this book. My own perspective is roughly that of Melanie Klein, who argues that love and hate are the basic categories of human experience. As an idealist, Klein (1975) believes we create these experiences out of our hopes and fears (Alford 1989). More recent work in the evolutionary basis of moral psychology seems to support Klein's argument. See especially Frans De Waal (1996), Robert Wright (1994), and James Q. Wilson (1993).

That humans see the world in fundamentally moral terms does not, of course, mean that they act morally or that these moral terms correspond to what we would ordinarily think of as "higher" morality. More on this in chapters 4 and 5.

6. Someone must have read it because the NRC rebuts it point by point in an unsigned report of March 3, 1978.

7. Atherton read this case study and says I should tell you that he now sleeps in a bed in a better apartment.

8. I do not know McGuire and did not interview him. This story is from a newspaper report.

9. Readers interested in more dramatic accounts should turn to Glazer and Glazer (1989) or Miethe (1999, 149–208).

10. How one might begin to change these realities is a crucial question but not my question. In "The False Dawn of Civil Society," David Rieff (1999) argues that it takes the power of the state to render the powerful private organization responsible to the public. True enough, and who remains to render the powerful public organization responsible to the public? Who watches the watchers?

THREE: WHISTLEBLOWERS' NARRATIVES

1. The same principle applies even within the world of texts. Langer (1991) compares diaries, written at the time or shortly after the experience, with more distant representations of the Holocaust, such as essays and a novel, also written by survivors. The essays and novel render the experience whole and comprehensible. That is, they mislead. The texts I have relied on most frequently are e-mails from whistleblowers, which are more like diaries than essays or novels.

2. Literary standards may mislead us into overvaluing narrative unity and coherence, all those things that contribute to a good story. Narrative – whether mine or the whistleblower's – gives meaning to experience. But is there any reason to assume that a meaningful account is any closer to the truth than an unmeaningful one? On the contrary, the truth is incoherent, manifested only in bits and pieces that don't fit together. Every narrative risks becoming the "forceful imposition of a story order upon human experience that is in itself disconnected, incoherent, and absurd" (Johnson 1993, 177). The most truthful witness of all may be the one who can't tell a coherent story about his or her experience, so that it remains in fragments, the real stuff of experience. This is why, according to Janet Malcolm (1999), that Sheila McGough, a lawyer accused of defrauding

her clients, was convicted – not because she was guilty but because she couldn't tell a coherent story about her innocence.

3. I have turned to the theory of narrative in order to think more systematically about whistleblower narratives. Most helpful was the work of William Labov (1972), a structural linguist, whose most famous work, *Language in the Inner City*, is a study of black English vernacular. I also turned to several narratologists, as they are called. Here I include the works of Maurice Blanchot (1995), Roland Barthes (1975), Gerald Prince (1987), Gérard Genette (1988), Algirdas Greimas (1983), and Mieke Bal (1997). The best definition of narratology is that of Genette (1988, 8), who says that narratology is distinguished by "respect for mechanisms of the text." This includes verbal texts, tales, and stories. One of the achievements of narratology is to demonstrate the sophistication of everyday narratives, which share almost every mechanism of the classic text. I turn to narratology as an adjunct to interpretation, not for the sake of the text but for the sake of understanding.

4. A fully developed narrative has the following elements according to Labov (1972, 362–70; Pratt 1977, 45–46):

a. Abstract (establishes the relationship to the listener)
b. Orientation (sets the context, time, place, persons)
c. Complicating action (then what happened)
d. Evaluation (what it all means, the point of the story)
e. Result or resolution (the ending)
f. Coda (closes the sequence of events, often returning to present)

No whistleblower narrative has all these elements, and there is no reason it should. Some elements are more important than others. The resolution is essential; the coda is not. Many whistleblowers' narratives have the quality of anecdotes, and that too is fine. What is missing in most whistleblower narratives is evaluation and resolution. Even an anecdote has to have a point. What is missing, in other words, is the meaning of the story as framed by its ending.

5. One could argue that the experience of being stuck in static time is itself an evaluation by whistleblowers. Several whistleblower comments, such as the one by the whistleblower who spoke of his life as "the turbulence of stagnant motion," support this claim. Overall, however, it was my experience that the dominance of chronology over plot that marks this theme was itself an alternative to evaluation, a way for the whistleblower to delay evaluating the narrative. In response, one might argue that

evaluation is not a question of motivation but of narrative structure. If the narrator communicates that the endless chronological sequence is pointless, that *is* an evaluation. Although this is true, it remains the case that the whistleblower works hard not to reach that conclusion. One sees this, for example, in the way in which narratives organized strictly by chronological time rarely change tense. Time travels only in one direction: from the past slowly forward into an ever-receding present. This makes it more difficult to gain even a little perspective on events.

6. The psychoanalyst Melanie Klein (1975) holds that paranoia is the first epistemological step in which we take our suffering inside and give it an outside cause against which we can safely rage. From this perspective, paranoia is the foundation of thought, the process by which we learn to categorize. Our first categories are good and bad: that which causes pleasure and that which causes pain. Any theory that connects experiences and events that are not contiguous, such as the effect of gamma rays on marigolds, has its roots in paranoia. Whether the paranoid is crazy is a matter of degree. Any imaginative artist or scientist needs a little paranoia.

7. Because Tom was protesting the military's failure to educate his son, he is technically not a whistleblower. Because Tom's case affects many others in the military, he comes close. In fact, this is probably why the military responded as it did. A fair amount of money is involved. See the case of Laura Bastion in chapter 2.

8. Martin Edwin Andersen asked that I use his real name. The quotation is from an e-mail titled "The Zen of Whistleblowing (Notes from 4:30 in the morning, one Sunday)."

9. Diegesis refers to the fictional world in which the situations and events that are narrated occur. It is fictional only in the sense that it stems from the subjective experience of the narrator. All worlds are fictional in this sense.

10. General George Lee Butler (Smith 1997, 20) attributed his remark to Flannery O'Connor.

FOUR: WHISTLEBLOWER ETHICS

1. I wrote a book about how narcissism might become moral, titled *Narcissism: Socrates, the Frankfurt School, and Psychoanalytic Theory* (Alford 1988). For those with a professional interest in the topic, I should state that I find Janine Chasseguet-Smirgel's (1984) account of narcissism the most compelling, in which she argues, following Béla Grunberger (1979), that the ego ideal is best seen as the avatar of primary narcissism. In thinking

about narcissism as inspiration or perversion (it is potentially always both), I find Kohut's (1985) account more compelling than Kernberg's (1985) in *Borderline Conditions and Pathological Narcissism*, though Kohut's idealization of narcissism exceeds my own.

2. Several studies of rescuers designate a subcategory of rescuer who acts not primarily out of care and concern but out of resistance to hated and hateful authority (Fogelman 1994, 118). Most whistleblowers seem to fit this general category, though one must be careful in separating care and concern from hatred of aggression, cruelty, and destructiveness. "Nice" emotions like care and concern do not necessarily have nice sources, nor should they.

3. Ron Ridenhour and I participated in a film project that became the documentary *Roots of Evil*, by Rex Bloomstein. I heard him say these things in interviews that ended up as outtakes from the documentary.

4. I have heard Lawrence Rockwood talk publicly and have spoken with him. My portrait draws from these experiences, as well as from Shacochis's (1999) book on the Haitian invasion, which devotes a chapter to Rockwood's story.

FIVE: IMPLICATIONS OF WHISTLEBLOWER ETHICS

1. Elmer Sprague (1967, 387) may just be describing a discipline, but he appears to be endorsing a position when he says about the moral sense that "the present day moral philosopher no longer casts his study as an investigation of ... a moral faculty, but rather as a study of the logic of moral discourse." As though these were the only choices: morality as mental faculty on the one hand, the analysis of discourse on the other.

2. Impartialism includes not only traditional Kantian, but also utilitarian, deontological, and consequentialist theories. However different these approaches, each identifies morality with a perspective of impartiality, impersonality, objectivity, and universality.

3. My argument here owes a great deal to an exchange of letters with Robert Fullinwider, who disagrees with what I say, which is why he has been so helpful.

4. As usual, these things are more complicated than a simple summary allows. That apostle of impartialism, Kant, had some good things to say about patriotism, an instance of loyalty which is nothing if not particular. In "Concerning the Common Saying: This May Be True in Theory but Does Not Apply to Practice," Kant (1949, 416–17) argues that patriotism allows people to better appreciate the humanity of their fellows and thus

treat them as universal citizens. But what about the humanity of those who are not one's fellow citizens? Doesn't patriotism make knowing this correspondingly more difficult? All good things do not fit neatly together. Because we admire patriotism does not mean that we can render it compatible with impartialism. Sometimes we have to choose.

5. In *The Inner Ocean: Individualism and Democratic Culture* (1992), Kateb defines democratic individualism, as he calls it, and which he much admires, in terms that come close indeed to what Arendt calls thought, as I point out in chapter 1. Individualism is about getting a little distance on oneself, as well as on one's world, so one can think about what one is doing almost as though one were talking with another who is doing it – almost another but not quite. "Autonomy consists in significant differentiation achieved through some distance between one and the world, and between one and oneself" (49). Has Kateb changed his mind since his 1984 work on Arendt? Or is individualism not as connected to morality as one might hope? My reading of *The Inner Ocean* suggests the latter. Individuality may foster empathy, but it is first of all about the individual who is oneself. My study of the origins of moral acts in wounded narcissism helps explain why some individuals might appear to give up so much for others.

6. Writing about Socrates' refusal to inflict an injustice for fear of damaging his relationship to himself, Hannah Arendt refers to the soundless dialogue (*eme emautō*) between me and myself (*Theaetetus*, 189e, *Sophist* 263e). Unlike Hippias, who cannot bear to talk with himself, Socrates listens to the other fellow who is waiting at home for him, his internal partner. If Socrates has done something that is shameful, his internal partner will not let him rest in peace. "Later times have given the fellow who awaits Socrates in his home the name of 'conscience.'" (Arendt 1978b, part 1, 190).

7. The emphasis is Arendt's; the internal quote is from Karl Jaspers.

8. Much as Habermas (1971) turned to the *telos* of truth inherent in language. We are always trying to find substitutes for our failed gods. But then again, this is how Freud defined the ego ideal.

9. Several works on rescuers use the term "universalistic" to characterize those who rescued Jews: they say they would have helped anyone (Oliner and Oliner 1988, 165–67; Tec 1986, 154). In fact, one might as well call rescuers particularistic: rescuers say they would have helped any particular person in need. All this shows how difficult it is to connect the practice of ethics with its theory. It also shows the need to let practice, not theory, lead the way, lest we make the ideal actor fit the ideal theory.

SIX: ORGANIZED THOUGHTLESSNESS

1. Some organizations, and some types of organizations, have far higher rates of whistleblowing than others. One wonders whether this has to do with the amount of wrongdoing or with how much whistleblowers fear retaliation. Using interview data from all employees in several different organizations, Miethe (1999, 61–67) concludes that rates of reporting observed wrongdoing vary dramatically (the second lowest level of reporting took place in a university administration). All organizations are not the same, and I do not mean to imply they are, any more than Weber means that all bureaucracies are the same: they are, and they're not. In "The Implications of an Organization's Structure on Whistleblowing," Granville King (1999) uncovers some important distinctions.

2. My account is from Vandivier's (1979) published article. I've changed the names of all the participants but Vandivier and R. G. Jeter, whose testimony is on record.

3. For Foucault (1980a), the leading instrument of disciplinary normalization is what he calls "the gaze." Foucault's father was a doctor, and that is perhaps the best way to explain his concept of the gaze (le regard) as a clinical method. The gaze represents the tacit observational principles of the experienced clinician, knowledgeable about individuality and particularity but uninterested in what goes on underneath, or inside, except as it is manifest as a change in the surface. The gaze is empirical, objective, and inductive, seeing the world in terms of categories and symptoms that may be classified and controlled. The gaze is the means by which knowledge becomes power. It is the methodology and ideology by which science and bureaucracy organize, classify, and control the world. My understanding of Foucault's view of power is indebted to Ansell-Pearson (1994).

4. See Brock's "Confessions of a Right Wing Hit Man," in Esquire 128 (July 1997).

5. Reynolds lists fifty-seven and a half Federal statutes. There are many more. Hundreds of state and local laws are on the books. I found Reynolds's manuscript helpful in many ways. Miethe (1999, 98–132) lists hundreds of federal and state laws.

6. To be sure, calls for new legislation are often included in "The Need for Reform," but new legislation is seldom central (Devine 1997, 153–54). In private discussions with whistleblower lawyers, new legislation gets even shorter shrift. Better enforcement of existing legislation and easier access to the courts are another matter.

151

7. Donald Rein is a pseudonym. U.S. District Court Judge Thomas Hogan is the judge's real name.

8. From a talk by Tom Devine, legal director of the Government Accountability Project, at the "Future of Whistleblowing" conference, Georgetown University, Washington, D.C., April 4 1998.

9. Arendt's (1958, 36, 186) concept of political action is often seen as a utopian idealization, the province of Greek heroes like Achilles and Pericles. It is an idealization she insufficiently discouraged, but it would miss her point to leave it at that. George Kateb (1984, 40–41) is not mistaken to state that Arendt sometimes idealizes politics for its own sake, so much so that the goals of politics become irrelevant. Relevant is only what political action can do for the political actor – save him or her from the meaninglessness of a merely private existence. Kateb calls this nihilism because the act is everything, the political goal nothing. In any case, I am using Arendt for the power of her critique, not the correctness of her ideals.

10. It is unsurprising that Arendt is a harsh critic of bureaucracy. What is surprising is the degree to which she assimilates totalitarianism, the banality of Adolf Eichmann's evil, mass society, and bureaucracy. Needless to say, ours is not a totalitarian society. None of the organizations within which whistleblowers have been employed have a totalitarian structure. None, not even the military, seeks the total coordination of all aspects of an employee's life, the *Gleichshaltung* (total coordination) of Nazi Germany. To control the employee's work life is enough. But Arendt does not define totalitarianism in terms of its structure, at least not directly. She defines it in terms of its eradication of individuality and plurality, signs of the common world. It is in this regard that she posits a connection between totalitarianism and bureaucracy, "something like a family resemblance; each category involves at least some parvenu features" (Pitkin 1998, 79). By the term "parvenu features," Pitkin means that each involves an identification with the aggressor, requiring that the parvenu deny his or her own situation, background, and circumstances – all the things that make individuals unique. The result is a terrible isolation and loneliness, leading the parvenu to cling ever more tightly to society.

11. Oliner and Oliner (1988, 169) point out that 80 percent of rescuers did not consult anyone before putting their lives and the lives of their entire families at risk. Some rescuers were caught, tortured, and killed, along with their entire families.

12. If one wanted, one could see the argument of my book as correcting two abstractions rampant in political theory: the abstract liberalism of

Kateb's (1992) *The Inner Ocean: Individualism and Democratic Culture*, and the abstract subjects of discipline perspective taken by Foucault.

13. Hirschman's (1970) position is a little more complicated. Applying an economic model to politics, Hirschman knows that an individual exiting a company by not buying its brand will of course not be noticed. But when Hirschman writes about resignation over matters of principle, he always presumes a political context. That is, he assumes that his exit will be noticed and his voice heard. This is mistaken. What is not mistaken is Hirschman's appreciation of voice, even when exit is easier.

SEVEN: THE POLITICAL THEORY OF SACRIFICE

1. I am taking liberties with Durkheim here, associating the "conscience collective" of *The Division of Labor in Society*, an early work, with his developed view of the sacred in *The Elementary Forms of Religious Life*, and elsewhere, where he does not use the term. Durkheim (1933, 80) believes that not much is left of the conscience collective, finding it in "only a very restricted part" of the psychic life of advanced societies. This, though, is a little misleading, for by the conscience collective Durkheim refers to a particular mode of social cohesion. That a latent sense of the sacred remains in modern societies, that it is widespread, not confined to the power centers of society, but based on the awe-inspiring distance between individual and society, are central tenets of his. It is in this sense that I am using the term "conscience collective."

References

Adorno, Theodor. 1974. *Minima Moralia: Reflections from Damaged Life.* Trans. E. F. N. Jephcott. London: NLB.

Alford, C. Fred. 1988. *Narcissism: Socrates, the Frankfurt School, and Psychoanalytic Theory.* New Haven: Yale University Press.

———. 1989. *Melanie Klein and Critical Social Theory.* New Haven: Yale University Press.

Ansell-Pearson, Keith. 1994. *An Introduction to Nietzsche as Political Thinker.* Cambridge: Cambridge University Press.

Arendt, Hannah. 1956. "What Is Freedom?" In *Between Past and Future: Eight Exercises in Political Thought,* enlarged ed., 143–72. Harmondsworth, England: Penguin Books.

———. 1958. *The Human Condition.* Chicago: University of Chicago Press.

———. 1964. *Eichmann in Jerusalem: A Report on the Banality of Evil.* Rev. and enlarged ed. New York: Viking Press.

———. 1968. "Isak Dinesen." In *Men in Dark Times.* New York: Harcourt, Brace and World.

———. 1973. *The Origins of Totalitarianism.* New York: Harcourt Brace.

———. 1978a. *The Jew as Pariah.* Ed. Ron H. Feldman. New York: Grove.

———. 1978b. *The Life of the Mind.* New York: Harcourt Brace.

———. 1997. *Rahel Varnhagen: The Life of a Jewess.* 1st complete ed. Ed. Liliane Weissberg, trans. Richard Winston and Clara Winston. Baltimore: Johns Hopkins University Press.

Bal, Mieke. 1997. *Narratology: Introduction to the Theory of Narrative.* 2d ed. Toronto: University of Toronto Press.

Barthes, Roland. 1975. "An Introduction to the Structural Analysis of Narrative." *New Literary History* 6: 237–62.

Bauman, Zygmunt. 1989. *Modernity and the Holocaust.* Ithaca, N.Y.: Cornell University Press.

———. 1991. *Modernity and Ambivalence.* Ithaca, N.Y.: Cornell University Press.

Benedict, Ruth. 1946. *The Chrysanthemum and the Sword: Patterns of Japanese Culture*. Boston: Houghton Mifflin.

Blanchot, Maurice. 1995. *The Writing of the Disaster*. Trans. Ann Smock. Lincoln: University of Nebraska Press.

Blum, Lawrence A. 1994. *Moral Perception and Particularity*. Cambridge: Cambridge University Press.

Brock, David. 1993. *The Real Anita Hill: The Untold Story*. New York: Free Press.

——. 1997. "Confessions of a Right Wing Hit Man." *Esquire* 128 (July).

Buber, Martin. 1965. *Between Man and Man*. Trans. R. G. Smith. New York: MacMillan. Reprint.

Chasseguet-Smirgel, Janine. 1984. *The Ego Ideal*. Trans. Paul Barrows. New York: Norton.

Chriss, James. 1998. "Review of Habermas, *Between Facts and Norms*." *Theory and Society* 27, no. 3: 417–25.

Clark, Charles. 1997. "Whistleblowers." *CQ Researcher* 7: 1057–80.

Darwall, Stephen. 1983. *Impartial Reason*. Ithaca, N.Y.: Cornell University Press.

Devine, Thomas. 1997. *The Whistleblower's Survival Guide: Courage without Martyrdom*. Washington, D.C.: Fund for Constitutional Government.

——. 1998. "Secrecy and Accountability in Scientific Research." *Forum for Applied Research and Public Policy* 13, no. 1: 65–70.

De Waal, Frans. 1996. *Good Natured: The Origins of Right and Wrong in Humans and Other Animals*. Cambridge: Harvard University Press.

Donagan, Alan. 1977. *The Theory of Morality*. Chicago: University of Chicago Press.

Douglas, Mary. 1966. *Purity and Danger: An Analysis of Concepts of Pollution and Taboo*. Harmondsworth, England: Penguin.

Durkheim, Emile. 1933. *The Division of Labor in Society*. Trans. George Simpson. New York: Macmillan.

——. 1965. *The Elementary Forms of Religious Life*. Trans. Joseph Ward Swain. New York: Free Press.

Elias, Norbert. 1994. *The Civilizing Process*. Trans. Edmund Jephcott. Oxford: Blackwell.

Elliston, Frederick, et al. 1985a. *Whistleblowing: Managing Dissent in the Workplace*. New York: Praeger.

——. 1985b. *Whistleblowing Research: Methodological and Moral Issues*. New York: Praeger.

Erikson, Erik. 1963. *Childhood and Society*. 2d ed. New York: Norton.

Fletcher, George. 1993. *Loyalty: An Essay on the Morality of Relationships*. New York: Oxford University Press.

Fogelman, Eva. 1994. *Conscience and Courage: Rescuers of Jews during the Holocaust.* New York: Doubleday.

Forster, E. M. 1927. *Aspects of the Novel.* London: Methuen.

Foucault, Michel. 1979. *Discipline and Punish: The Birth of the Prison.* Trans. Alan Sheridan. New York: Vintage Books.

———. 1980a. "The Eye of Power." In *Power/Knowledge: Selected Interviews and Other Writings, 1972–1977,* ed. Colin Gordon, 146–65. New York: Pantheon Books.

———. 1980b. "Prison Talk." In *Power/Knowledge: Selected Interviews and Other Writings, 1972–1977,* ed. Colin Gordon, 37- 54. New York: Pantheon Books.

Freud, Anna. 1966. *The Ego and the Mechanisms of Defense.* Rev. ed. New York: International Universities Press. Vol. 2 of *The Writings of Anna Freud.*

Freud, Sigmund. 1908. "Creative Writers and Day-Dreaming." In *The Standard Edition of the Complete Psychological Works of Sigmund Freud,* ed. James Strachey. London: Hogarth Press, 1953–74, 24 vols., vol. 9, 141–56.

———. 1914. "On Narcissism." In *The Standard Edition of the Complete Psychological Works of Sigmund Freud,* ed. James Strachey. London: Hogarth Press, 1953–74, 24 vols., vol. 14, 67–104.

———. 1961. *Civilization and Its Discontents.* Trans. James Strachey. New York: Norton.

Genette, Gérard. 1988. *Narrative Discourse Revisited.* Trans. Jane Lewin. Ithaca, N.Y.: Cornell University Press.

Gilligan, Carol. 1982. *In a Different Voice: Psychological Theory and Women's Development.* Cambridge: Harvard University Press.

Girard, René. 1977. *Violence and the Sacred.* Trans. Patrick Gregory. Baltimore: Johns Hopkins University Press.

Glazer, Myron Peretz, and Penina Migdal Glazer. 1989. *The Whistleblowers.* New York: Basic Books.

Gordon, Suzanne. 1999. "Unfairly Targeting RNs." *Boston Globe,* January 8, 1999, A19.

Greimas, Algirdas. 1983. *Structural Semantics: An Attempt at Method.* Trans. Daniele McDowell et al. Lincoln: University of Nebraska Press.

Grunberger, Béla. 1979. *Narcissism: Psychoanalytic Essays.* Trans. Joyce Diamanti. New York: International Universities Press.

Habermas, Jürgen. 1971. *Knowledge and Human Interests.* Trans. Jeremy Shapiro. Boston: Beacon Press.

———. 1984. *The Theory of Communicative Action.* Trans. Thomas McCarthy. 2 vols. Boston: Beacon Press.

——. 1996. *Between Facts and Norms: Contributions to a Discourse Theory of Law and Democracy.* Trans. William Rehg. Cambridge: MIT Press.

Hallie, Philip. 1979. *Lest Innocent Blood Be Shed: The Story of the Village of Le Chambon.* New York: Harper & Row.

Hirschman, Albert O. 1970. *Exit, Voice, and Loyalty: Responses to Decline in Firms, Organizations, and States.* Cambridge: Harvard University Press.

Jackall, Robert. 1988. *Moral Mazes.* New York: Oxford University Press.

Johnson, Mark. 1993. *Moral Imagination.* Chicago: University of Chicago Press.

Johnston, David Day. 1999. "On Tax Day, I.R.S. Prepared to Fire Star Whistle-Blower." *New York Times,* April 17, A1.

Jos, Philip, Mark Tompkins, and Steven Hays. 1989. "In Praise of Difficult People: A Portrait of the Committed Whistleblower." *Public Administration Review* 49: 552–61.

Jubb, Peter. 1999. "Whistleblowing: A Restrictive Definition and Interpretation." *Journal of Business Ethics* 21: 77–94

Kafka, Franz. 1971. "In the Penal Colony." In *The Complete Stories and Parables,* ed. Nahum Glatzer, 140–67. New York: Quality Paperback Book Club.

Kant, Immanuel. 1949. "Concerning the Common Saying: This May Be True in Theory but Does Not Apply to Practice." In *The Philosophy of Kant,* trans. Carl Friedrich, 412–29. New York: Modern Library.

Kateb, George. 1984. *Hannah Arendt: Politics, Conscience, Evil.* Totowa, N.J.: Rowman and Allanheld.

——. 1992. *The Inner Ocean: Individualism and Democratic Culture.* Ithaca, N.Y.: Cornell University Press.

Kernberg, Otto. 1985. *Borderline Conditions and Pathological Narcissism.* Northvale, N.J.: Jason Aronson.

Kierkegaard, Søren. 1957. *The Concept of Dread.* Trans. Walter Lowrie. Princeton: Princeton University Press.

King, Granville. 1999. "The Implications of an Organization's Structure on Whistleblowing." *Journal of Business Ethics* 20: 315–26.

Klein, Melanie. 1975. "Notes on Some Schizoid Mechanisms." In *Envy and Gratitude and Other Essays.* Vol. 3 of *The Writings of Melanie Klein,* ed. R. E. Money-Kyrle, 1–24. New York: Free Press.

Kohlberg, Lawrence. 1976. "Moral Stages and Moralization: The Cognitive-Developmental Approach." In *Moral Development and Behavior,* ed. T. Lickona. New York: Holt, Rinehart & Winston.

Kohn, Alfie. 1990. *The Brighter Side of Human Nature: Altruism and Empathy in Everyday Life.* New York: Basic Books.

Kohut, Heinz. 1985. "Forms and Transformations of Narcissism." In *Self Psychology and the Humanities: Reflections on a New Psychoanalytic Approach*, ed. Charles Strozier, 97–123. New York: Norton.

Labov, William. 1972. *Language in the Inner City: Studies in the Black English Vernacular.* Philadelphia: University of Pennsylvania Press.

Ladd, John. 1967. "Loyalty." In *The Encyclopedia of Philosophy*, ed. Paul Edwards, vol. 5. New York: Macmillan and Free Press.

Langer, Lawrence. 1991. *Holocaust Testimonies: The Ruins of Memory.* New Haven: Yale University Press.

Lasch, Christopher. 1995. *The Revolt of the Elites and the Betrayal of Democracy.* New York: Norton.

Lear, Jonathan. 1990. *Love and Its Place in Nature: A Philosophical Interpretation of Freudian Psychoanalysis.* New Haven: Yale University Press.

Lukes, Stephen. 1973. *Individualism.* Oxford: Basil Blackwell.

Levi, Primo. 1988. *The Drowned and the Saved.* Trans. Raymond Rosenthal. New York: Summit Books.

Lewis, Michael. 1992. *Shame: The Exposed Self.* New York: Free Press.

Lifton, Robert Jay. 1986. *The Nazi Doctors: Medical Killing and the Psychology of Genocide.* New York: Basic Books.

Malcolm, Janet. 1999. *The Crime of Sheila McGough.* New York: Knopf.

Marcuse, Herbert. 1969. *An Essay on Liberation.* Boston: Beacon Press.

———. 1978. *The Aesthetic Dimension: Toward a Critique of Marxist Aesthetics.* Boston: Beacon Press.

Miceli, Marcia, and Janet Near. 1992. *Blowing the Whistle: The Organizational and Legal Implications for Companies and Employees.* New York: Lexington Books.

Miethe, Terance. 1999. *Whistleblowing at Work: Tough Choices in Exposing Fraud, Waste, and Abuse on the Job.* Boulder, Colo.: Westview Press.

Milgram, Stanley. 1974. *Obedience to Authority.* New York: Harper & Row.

Monroe, Kristen Renwick. 1996. *The Heart of Altruism: Perceptions of a Common Humanity.* Princeton, N.J.: Princeton University Press.

Murdoch, Iris. 1970. *The Sovereignty of Good.* London: Routledge.

Noddings, Nel. 1984. *Caring: A Feminist Perspective on Ethics and Education.* Berkeley: University of California Press.

Oliner, Samuel, and Pearl Oliner. 1988. *The Altruistic Personality: Rescuers of Jews in Nazi Europe.* New York: Free Press.

Orwell, George. 1949. *Nineteen Eighty-Four.* New York: Signet.

Orwin, Clifford. 1994. *The Humanity of Thucydides.* Princeton, N.J.: Princeton University Press.

Perlstein, Linda. 1998. "PEER." *Washington Post*, August 31, A19.

Phillips, Don. 1998. "FAA Missed Warning on Insulation Burn Test." *Washington Post*, November 8, A1.

Pitkin, Hanna. 1998. *The Attack of the Blob: Hannah Arendt's Concept of the Social.* Chicago: University of Chicago Press.

Pratt, Mary Louise. 1977. *Toward a Speech Act Theory of Literary Discourse.* Bloomington: Indiana University Press.

Prince, Gerald. 1987. *A Dictionary of Narratology.* Lincoln: University of Nebraska Press.

Putnam, Robert. 2000. *Bowling Alone: The Collapse and Revival of American Community.* New York: Simon and Schuster.

Rawls, John. 1971. *A Theory of Justice.* Cambridge: Harvard University Press, Belknap Press.

Reynolds, Ern. 1998. "Whistleblower Remedies: Counseling the Principled Dissenter." Unpublished.

Rieff, David. 1999. "The False Dawn of Civil Society." *Nation*, February 22, pp. 11–16.

Rothschild, Joyce, and Terance Miethe. 1996. "Keeping Organizations True to Their Purposes: The Role of Whistleblowing in Organizational Accountability and Effectiveness." Final Report to the Aspen Institute.

Rousseau, Jean-Jacques. 1964. "Discourse on the Origin and Foundations of Inequality among Men [Second Discourse]." In *The First and Second Discourses*, trans. R. Masters and J. Masters, 77–228. New York: St. Martin's Press.

Royce, Josiah. 1971. *The Philosophy of Loyalty.* New York: Hafner. c. 1908; facsimile of 1924 ed.

Sagan, Eli. 1988. *Freud, Women, and Morality: The Psychology of Good and Evil.* New York: Basic Books.

Sennett, Richard. 1998. *The Corrosion of Character: The Personal Consequences of Work in the New Capitalism.* New York: Norton.

Shacochis, Bob. 1999. *The Immaculate Invasion.* New York: Viking.

Shils, Edward. 1975. "Charisma, Order, and Status." In *Center and Periphery*, 256–75. Chicago: University of Chicago Press.

———. 1982. *The Constitution of Society.* Chicago: University of Chicago Press.

Smith, R. Jeffrey. 1997. "The General's Conscience: Why Nuclear Warrior George Lee Butler Changed His Mind." *Washington Post Magazine*, December 7.

Sprague, Elmer. 1967. "Moral Sense." In *The Encyclopedia of Philosophy*, ed. Paul Edwards, vol. 5, p. 387. New York: Macmillan and Free Press.

Strayer, Joseph. 1965. "Feudalism in Western Europe." In *Feudalism in History*, ed. Rushton Coulborn, 15–25. Hamden, Conn.: Archon Books. Reprint of 1956 Princeton University Press ed.

Strayer, Joseph, and Rushton Coulborn. 1965. "The Idea of Feudalism." In *Feudalism in History*, ed. Rushton Coulborn, 3–11. Hamden, Conn.: Archon Books. Reprint of 1956 Princeton University Press ed.

Tallis, Raymond. 1995. *Not Saussure: A Critique of Post-Saussurean Literary Theory*. 2d ed. London: Macmillan.

Tec, Nechama. 1986. *When Light Pierced the Darkness: Christian Rescue of Jews in Nazi-Occupied Poland*. New York: Oxford University Press.

Turner, Stephen. 1999. "The Significance of Shils." *Sociological Theory* 17, no. 2: 125–45.

Vandivier, Kermit. 1979. " 'Why Should My Conscience Bother Me?' " In *Life in Organizations: Workplaces as People Experience Them*, ed. R. M. Kanter and B. A. Stein. New York: Basic Books.

Weber, Max. 1946. *From Max Weber: Essays in Sociology*. Ed. H. H. Gerth and C. Wright Mills. New York: Oxford University Press.

Weisman, Jonathan. 1997. "Shut Down." *Washington Post*, July 6.

Wilson, James Q. 1993. *The Moral Sense*. New York: Free Press.

Winnicott, D. W. 1958. *Collected Papers: Through Paediatrics to Psycho-Analysis*. New York: Basic Books.

Wright, Robert. 1994. *The Moral Animal: Evolutionary Psychology and Everyday Life*. New York: Vintage Books.

Index